Mrs

Jam Today & Jams Tomorrow

Christine Gledhill

FLAG Publishing Ltd

Mrs G's Jam Today & Jams Tomorrow

First Published in June 2007

British Library Cataloguing in Publication Data
A catalogue record of this book is available from the British Library

ISBN 0 954 66622 4

Published by:

FLAG Publishing Ltd
Kempsey
Worcester
WR5 3JX
U.K.

Set in Lucida Sans, 10/14 pt by FLAG Publishing

Printed by Printright Ltd., Norton, Worcester

INTRODUCTION & ACKNOWLEDGEMENTS

I am always asked, "How long have you been making jam?' My reply is, "All my life!", or so it seems.

I think that if the truth be told the art of making jam has always been there in my background. My mother always seemed to be able to make something out of nothing ... or nothing that seemed relevant! We were living, as a family, in central India over the years of World War 2 and my earliest recollection of mum making jam was using a purple, hairy-leafed plant, rather like a nettle, that grew outside the back door of our house. I have never been able to find anyone who knows what the plant was really called but I recall that in my childhood the jam made from it was called "Pat-Wa Jam". Perhaps a local name for the plant but I do not know for certain.

When we returned to England, we went to live in my father's childhood home. My Nana had always said that if you were to plant a tree in the garden then it should be a fruit bearing variety. Therefore, I grew up in a garden full of apple, pear and plum trees, and with the ripened blackberries in the hedgerows of the Downs in the autumn and a mother who always made something from the fruits we children gathered, it is no small wonder that I inherited a love of making jam.

I followed my Nana's sound advice and when I finally settled in leafy Worcestershire, I filled my big garden with a mini orchard. Fruit trees do take time to grow and then bear fruit and I needed fruits to make my jams. I had learned the art of `scrumping' as a child, so I filled my store cupboard with damsons, blackberries, apples, wild plums and other fruits gathered from the country hedgerows, while I patiently waited on my own fruit trees growing.

INTRODUCTION & ACKNOWLEDGEMENTS

And grow they did. Twenty five years later, I gave away my fruit by the basketful, but in the intervening years I always had a store cupboard filled with jars of jams and bottled fruit that were used and replenished as the seasons passed each year.

When my children grew up and moved away from home I still made jar upon jar of jams from my orchard but then I started to wonder what I was going to do with all of my jam. My children often came home to visit me and inevitably went away with a load of jars containing my jams. I also provided jam for the local church fete and other such events but still I ended up with an excess.

It was the brother of one of our church members who sent his sister to ask me for some more of `Mrs Gledhill's plum jam' that made me realise that there was a market out there for good quality food. So I set off on the trail that I have now been following for the past 20 years or so. I decided though that my jams were not going to be just ordinary jam. I also knew that many country folk did what I had always done and made their own jams by using the well-known fruits and I wanted to invent my own special jams.

At one period of my adult life, I had lived in the West Indies, where the local dairy sold the most delicious ice-cream and they kept ahead of the local competition by producing a new flavour each and every month. I decided that I would emulate their innovative marketing strategy and try to produce a new addition to my range of jams every so often. That, quite frankly, is where the fun has come in. Sometimes my ideas have been generated by seeing the fruits on the hedgerows. Sometimes my customers feed me with an idea, occasionally I get the idea of a `name' that sounds intriguing and then I try to generate a preserve that fits the title. On other occasions I will have read something that starts me thinking "that's an idea".

This does sometimes result in a mistake but always my fertile brain will make something out of the idea and I will then sell the result to my customers along with the relevant anecdote or story. If the jam is sufficiently different, I will ask my customers for feedback and I do receive some lovely letters from folk.

I have built up a font of tales to tell, and, as my brother says, I can "bore for England, about Jam!", but then he is not averse to feeding me with ideas for "new flavours"!

Folk query my passion for creating preserves and even I wonder what feeds my motivation. Making jam is a world away from my professional career, which is, or was until I retired recently, teaching Mathematics, but my obsession with preserves has provided my sanity when the classroom got too hot for comfort. There is a certain joy in seeing lots of shiny jars of brightly-coloured preserves sitting on my shelves. I thrive on the accolades that my jam has been given by my friends and customers alike. Nowadays, with there being such a dearth of good, unadulterated food available on the market, I make the justification for my passion for jam as being on a one-woman crusade to show the world what good food should taste like. It certainly does not need to be filled with chemicals. Our grandmothers and their mothers before them, made their own jam with the fruits they could gather and some sugar. The results kept in store from one year to the next without the use of refrigeration.

My cry is “Let's get back to good quality food, properly made and stored and tasting of the fruit from which it is made”.

Jam making is a dying art and I want to keep that tradition alive for tomorrow.

INTRODUCTION & ACKNOWLEDGEMENTS

My own children are as besotted as I am with my jam. Their lifestyles do not let them get as involved as I have done but they have insisted that I must write all my knowledge down so that when they have the time, then...

But time is never available to them, so rather than let all I have achieved be lost to posterity, to quote Viola in Twelfth Night,

"*Lady, you are the cruel'st she alive,*

If you will lead these graces to the grave,

And leave the world no copy."

So this book is my inheritance for my grandchildren; for Leila, Leonie, Asher, Kallum, Cala, Dechlan, Ashlee-Rose and for the little one who did not make it, the special, wee fellow Lachlan.

I hope that one day the old skills will once again be part of ordinary life.

In the meantime, I hope that you will enjoy trying out some of my recipes. I wish you as much joy in preparing them as I have had in devising them.

You have jam today and jams for tomorrow.

Christine Gledhill
June 2007

Worcestershire

TEXTURES

One of the things that have always intrigued me is the texture of jams and marmalades.

I am always being asked, what makes a jam; what makes a preserve; what makes a conserve; or, what makes a jelly?

When you are making preserves, a simple rule of thumb is that you need to soften the fruit before you add the sugar, otherwise the resulting mixture tends to be more crystallised fruit in syrup. This is particularly important when dealing with hard fruits, like many of the citrus types. The softer, or wetter, the fruit then the more chances there are that the fruit will soften in the syrup. Strawberries, for example, will soften and almost disappear, when cooked.
In general, cook the fruit and then add the sugar.
Normally, fruit will stay intact if the sugar is added before any cooking takes place, so if you want chunky fruits then this is the route to take, but you may need to cook your mixture longer to get it to set properly.

With citrus fruits, there is an extra stage in the making.
If you want to have a smooth citrus jam then you need to cook the fruit and then homogenise it. I put the fruit into my food processor, after I have cooked it for about 45 minutes, and give it a good blend to liquidise the fruit.
This is also true for curds, “No bits” Marmalade, Marmelo etc.
Conversely, if you want to retain the texture of the fruit, chop it before cooking. Examples of this are found in almost all marmalades, pineapple and lemon jams, and virtually all chutneys.

IS IT A CHUTNEY, A PICKLE OR A TRACKLEMENT?

What is the difference?

This is yet another enigma, which does not have a definitive answer. As much as anything it is answered quite simply, by the comment "What's in a name?"

To me, chutney implies something fruity and rather sweet to the taste, which tends to be eaten with cheese. A pickle is made from vegetables and is usually eaten with meats.
However, even this definition falls very short of being correct and explicit, because many types of chutney are eaten with cold meat and what about "cheese and pickle sandwiches"? Where do they fit in?
Thus, I name my creations by what sounds right for them and hopefully my customers do not worry too much about any rigid definitions for any of my recipes. They enjoy them for what they are - well made and full of flavour!

I feel that chutney and pickle are interchangeable but they both fit well when eaten with cheeses or cold meats. Tracklements, on the other hand, are sweet complements that should be served with hot food, and in particular, meats. Many are used as glazes, which are smeared on the meat before it is cooked, and the flavours permeate through the meat during the cooking process.
I know many folk who will add a tracklement to the gravy as they make it and then serve this wonderful concoction with the Sunday joint.

So, does it really matter what it is called - enjoy the flavours and enjoy the fact that you, your family and friends are enjoying something that you have made - with love and care added as extra ingredients.

TESTING FOR A SET

Throughout all these recipes, I have made comment about "test for a set". I feel that I should explain a little about this important part of the jam making process.

For anyone who is new to jam-making "testing for a set" is probably a complete puzzle and something of a mystery. There are however many ways of doing this. The method I prefer is to drop about half a teaspoonful of the `juice' of the mixture onto a cold surface and examine the results. A clean saucer from the crockery cupboard is what I use. Leave your dollop of mixture for a few minutes to cool then push the `puddle' from the edge towards the centre, if it wrinkles then your jam will set. If it doesn't wrinkle then raise the temperature of the pan and boil the mixture for a little longer; testing it again a few minutes later.

A school of thought says that the heat under the mixture should be turned off while you are waiting for your test to cool. I have found that if you do have to reheat the mixture in order to the reach the correct "setting" temperature, it does take that much longer, so instead I turn the heat down to the lowest possible setting.

There is a more fool proof method of achieving a good "set" and that is to use a jam, or sugar, thermometer.
Jam, because of its high sugar content, will boil at a much higher temperature than water. If you choose to use a jam thermometer then make sure that the bulb is placed in the centre of the pan, (turn the heat down first so that the whole mixture is about the same temperature).
The temperature of the mixture needs to reach 220°F (104°C) to ensure a good set.

TESTING FOR A SET

This method will give a set with jellies or preserves that have a high matrix to solids ratio but it is sometimes difficult to achieve with thicker mixtures (marmalades).
If you are subsequently going to use alcohol-based ingredients, you will need a slightly higher temperature.

A useful tip to get a well-set jam with very little fuss is to use the pectin sugars that are readily available in supermarkets. I will often use half-granulated, or preserving, and half pectin sugar with mixtures of fruits. This is particularly useful with the "laced jams". Many mixtures benefit from not being overcooked, in terms of colour and taste, and many fruits are commercially grown by the hydroponics methods, consequently, as a result they have higher water content than those plants grown in the soil.

Do remember that the life of any preserve does depend directly on the temperature that it reaches when cooking, pectin aids the set but too much pectin does reduce the shelf life of the finished product.

WEIGHTS AND MEASURES

All of the weights and measures given in the recipes are in imperial units. Other measures of quantity that are used, such as teaspoon and tablespoon, are also used as these utensils are readily available to the cook in their own kitchen. No need for fancy measuring jugs - which only add to the washing up.

Given the very nature of the jam making process, there is often a need to give a best guess as to what quantity is required and sometimes personal taste means less or more of spices, for example. Experimentation is the key.

For the die-hard metric user, the table below gives approximate conversions from the measures used in the recipes.

As with all recipes do not mix the units, if you start with imperial, stay with imperial and never combine the two systems.

For liquid measures :-

1 teaspoon (tsp)	=	about 5 millilitre (ml)
2 teaspoons	=	1 dessertspoon
3 teaspoons	=	1 tablespoon (tbs)
5 tablespoons	=	half a cup or half a wineglass
10 tablespoons	=	1 cup or 1 wineglass = 6 fluid ozs

For weight measures :-

1 ounce (oz)	=	28 grams (g)
4 ounces (ozs)	=	113 grams
8 ounces (ozs)	=	226 grams (1/4 of a kilo)
16 ounces (ozs)	=	0.453 kilogramme
35 ounces (ozs)	=	1 kilogramme

APPLE AND GINGER

Ginger, when added to a jam gives it bite and piquancy but because it has such a strong taste in its own right, you have to be careful that your "carrier" complements and does not clash. Apples are a good base.
I do not find that powdered ginger is as effective as using a combination of shredded root and crystallised ginger, but even they have created problems for me.
I once received a terse letter from one very irate customer demanding to know what "this is". The "this" was flagged up in his original letter, which had never arrived, so my customer duly sent a second, even more irritated letter, along with a copy of the original letter but without the offending item. The only thing that I could presume was that he had found, in his jam, a chunk of root ginger and he had assumed that "this" was a "foreign body". Needless to say I have never heard back from him in response to my reply which explained my thoughts on the matter, so I've often wondered whether I was right in my assumption.

You will need

4¼ lbs of prepared apples
4 ozs of root ginger (freshly grated)
2 dessert spoons of chopped crystallised ginger
2 pints of water
4¼ lbs of sugar

APPLE AND GINGER

Method

When you are preparing the apples, cook the peel and cores in a small amount of water and rub this through a wire sieve into your jelly pan, the extra pectin assists the set. Discard the residue.
Add the water, the prepared apples and both the gingers and cook slowly until the apples have fluffed up. This will take about 20 minutes.

Add the sugar and bring back to boiling point, keep it at this temperature and stir frequently until the mixture has turned a deep russet colour.

This should take about an hour. Test for a set. When the jam is ready give it a short sharp fast boil for two or three minutes.

Pour the jam into clean dry jars and seal them immediately.

This will make about eight pounds of a beautiful rich coloured jam that will keep for up to a year.

APRICOT AND WALNUT

To my mind this is one of the nicest of jams. I think it is because of the texture.

When I first made up this recipe, I had taken some of it with me when I went to visit some friends in America, and Nanny insisted that I made her some of my "English scones". After a supermarket foray to acquire the ingredients, I made some plain scones that were promptly demolished along with my Apricot and Walnut jam. What a treat! Even I was impressed with the combination! I do not know what the difference between American and English flour is but that was a tea fit for a King!

It also scores well because it is one jam that can be made at any time of the year and, as such, can be made when the jam supplies run low. Not that that is such an advantage as it would have been in our Grandmother's day, as there are now freezers in most homes and fruit is readily available throughout the year.

You will need

1 lb of dried apricots, soaked overnight in water
2 good sized oranges
4¼ lbs of sugar
3 ozs of raisins
3 ozs of walnuts, chopped small

APRICOT AND WALNUT

Method

Soak the apricots overnight in about 2 pints of water and in the morning they should be soft. Chop them roughly, for this makes for a more uniform jam!
Cut the oranges across and then cut the halves into about five strips, then cut these strips into thin slices.

Put the apricots and oranges using the water that the apricots were soaked in, into an aluminium pan and cook slowly for about 45 minutes. Keep it stirred or it will stick and burn.
Add the sugar and bring back to boiling point, maintain it at boiling point for a further half an hour or until you can get a good set with the "juice".
Add the raisins and maintain the temperature for a further 15 minutes to swell the raisins.
Add the chopped walnuts and bring back to boiling point.
Turn off the heat and let the jam cool for about 5 minutes (this ensures an even distribution of raisins and walnuts through the jam): stir well and pour into clean dry jars and seal.

This will make about eight pounds of delicious jam that will keep for nine months or more if you can hide it somewhere cool and dark! But don't expect it to still be there when you next look for some, especially, if you tell the family where it is kept, because the jam will mysteriously appear on their tea table the next time you visit!

BLACKBERRIES IN WHISKEY

It seemed that I was always being asked to make blackberry jam, but not with apple, just blackberries! Somehow, it did not work for me but I am always open to suggestions. One time I was in the Jameson Heritage Centre in Ireland and there they had Blackberries in Jameson's Irish whiskey. Needless to say that this was enough to inspire me and when I came home I experimented and produced a jam that has proved to be very popular. Why it works in the way that it does, I do not know, but somehow Jameson's Irish whiskey makes a lovely creamy jam. The complement of flavours is 'right'. It does not work with Scotch nor with many other Irish whiskeys but it certainly does with Jameson's.

You will need

3 lbs of good blackberries
1 pint of water
3 lbs of pectin sugar
6 tablespoonfuls of Jameson's Irish whiskey

BLACKBERRIES IN WHISKEY

Method

Boil the blackberries in the water for about half an hour. Add the sugar and bring back to the boil, maintaining it at boiling point for a further 15 minutes when you should be able to get a good set.
Turn off the heat and leave the pan to cool for 20 to 30 minutes but stir the jam occasionally to prevent a skin forming.
Measure the whiskey into the pan and stir it well in.

Common sense will indicate how long to leave your preserve before adding the alcohol. If the jam is too hot the alcohol will fizzle and boil off, if you leave it too long then you run the risk of the jam not keeping. Do remember that the cooling depends on the temperature of the kitchen and the shape of your pan.

Pour the jam into clean dry jars and seal as quickly as possible.

This will make 5½ to 6 lb of delicious jam. It will happily keep for a year, if you do not eat it in the meantime. As with all jams, store it in a cool dark place.

Note
Pick your blackberries early in September rather than in October, as they are firmer and have a better flavour then. Blackberries freeze well if they are washed, then drained, dried and then packed into plastic bags. They can be kept in the freezer for using later in the year. It is well worth picking extra fruit, storing it and making this recipe up as and when you want it.

BLACKBERRY AND APPLE

I am always asked "What is your best seller?"

Undoubtedly my answer is the one that everyone used to make and everyone remembers from Granny's store-cupboard but for some reason it is not made as a commercial jam by the jam manufacturers.

I often wonder why but I do know that once the blackberries ripen on the hedgerows, I find it hard to keep up with the demand for this traditional jam. The subliminal desires are triggered off and I have to keep my customers satisfied.
In September, I travel with boxes at the ready in my car and spend many thoughtful hours picking the shiny fruits. There is something special about a box full of blackberries.
Is it that they are free of charge? Is it the richness of the colour? Is it just being out on the last of the summer days before winter sets in? Or is it about going back to childhood when we roamed freely over the Downs, sent out by Mother and needed only to return when the box was full of fruits?
I don't know which but it is a jam full of memories for me and it would seem full of childhood memories for my customers.

You will need

2¼ lbs of blackberries,
2¼ lbs of cooking apples
4¼ lbs of sugar
2 pints of water

BLACKBERRY AND APPLE

Method

Make sure that your blackberries are bug-free because in some autumns the fruits are covered with tiny spiders but a quick wash in salty water will clear them off. Do not forget to rinse the remains of the salty water off your fruit before you start to cook with them.

Put the blackberries in a pan with the water and cook for about 30 minutes. Pour the contents of your pan into a fine metal sieve over your preserving pan and, using the back of a wooden spoon; rub the fruit against the sieve until the 'trash' left in the sieve looks dry. It is worth putting some effort into this as the pulp of the blackberries adds to the final flavour of the jam. Discard the residue in the sieve.

Peel the apples and cut into quarters so that you can remove the cores. Put the quartered apples into the blackberry juice and bring to the boil. Maintain it at a simmer point until you can smash the apples to a pulp. (I use the same tool that I use for mashing potatoes). Add the sugar and then raise the temperature to boil the jam rapidly until you get a good set. The quicker this can be achieved the better are the colour and the taste. Pour, when ready, into clean, dry jars and seal immediately.

This will make about eight pounds of jam that will keep for more than a year providing it is kept in a cool dark place.

Note:

You can use raspberries instead of blackberries but if I do, I do not take the pips out.

I boil the apple peelings and cores in some water, then rub them through a sieve, and use this (pectin rich) juice to cook both the apples and raspberries in.

If using raspberries that are "full and fleshy", swap half your sugar for Pectin sugar as you jam will set quicker and will be a better colour. This makes a good looking, bright pink, jam that tastes equally as good as the blackberry recipe.

CHERRY AND BLACKCURRANT MARMALADE

What is marmalade and what is jam?
That is a question that I am always being asked but I think, after some thought, that it is a more of a matter of what sounds right. This recipe is nice too, but one I devised by accident and not by intention.
My neighbours had a cherry tree (Prunus avium) and once upon a time they gave me a bucket full of the fruits to see what I could do with them. Cherry cheese sounded nice, so I set off cooking the cherries but got distracted and forgot about them until they had gone past the point of being suitable for my original intentions. Never being one for rejecting anything without trying to use the fruit in an alternative endeavour, I found some blackcurrants in my freezer and set about creating a jam from them and the spoiled cherries. Bingo! I had recovered a success from potential failure.
I have made it many times since but have not had to spoil the cherries first and it has been equally successful. Here is the unspoiled version.

You will need

2½ lbs Cherries* (or 2½ lbs of dessert cherries, after stoning)
2½ lbs of Blackcurrants
4½ lb of sugar
1½ pints of water

CHERRY AND BLACKCURRANT MARMALADE

Method

Cook the cherries in the water and leave to cool.
Remove the stones by rubbing the fruits through your fingers in the pan. Add the blackcurrants and bring to the boil. Cook for about 20 minutes.
Add the sugar and return to the boil.
Boil rapidly until you get a good set.
Pour into clean jars and seal.

* The Prunus Cherries are fruits that are about the shape and size of a small grape and a purple colour. The fruits of the copper-leaved, flowering cherry have quite a large, flat stone.

An alternative recipe - **BLACKCURRANTS IN KIRSCH**
This is another good jam made with blackcurrants but replace the cherries (in the above) with about 2 lb of prepared apples.
Cook the apples in an extra half pint of water until they are light and fluffy add the blackcurrants and cook until all the fruits are soft, This will take about 20 minutes.
Add the sugar and bring to the boil maintaining this temperature for a further 20 minutes. Test for a set.
When a set is reached, leave the jam to cool for 20 minutes or so then add about 5 fluid ounces of cherry brandy; stir in well and then pour into clean dry jars. Seal quickly.
Both recipes will make about eight pounds of jam that will have a shelf life of about 10 months, if kept cool and in a dark place.

DAMSON JAM (OR GREENGAGE)

To my mind, Damson makes the king of jams. It can be eaten on scones, each with a heap of cream on top. The sharp, full flavour of the damson is a perfect complement to cream and makes for a very English tea time.
But we are now part of Europe, so I now offer something different. Consider eating it with Brie cheese? Try it; it is quite sensational, especially with butter puffs, good brie and a pot of damson jam. It is food fit for any international get-together. Alternatively serve hot deep-fried Brie with a blob of this jam melting over the top, with toast and a green salad.
The complementary creamy nature of the cheese and sharpness of this jam must be the common denominator of these three ideas.

You will need

4¼ lbs of Damsons (or Greengages)
4¼ lbs of sugar
1½ pints of water with the damsons, but only one pint is needed for the greengage version of this jam

DAMSON JAM (OR GREENGAGE)

Method

Cook the damsons in the water for about half and hour and then remove the stones.*
Add the sugar, raise the temperature and boil rapidly until you get a good set.

Pour the jam into clean dry jars and seal immediately. This will make about eight pounds of a deep purple and very delicious jam. It will keep for a good year if kept cool and dark ... And, of course, if you do not eat it before the time expires.

** My tip, to save wasting the fruit, is to count the number of damsons into the pan, so that when cooked and allowed to cool, I don a pair of latex rubber gloves and take the stones out by hand, counting them out! It is boring, keeping count, but you end up with a more fruity jam.*

GREENGAGES are old fashioned fruits that are not readily available over the counter in shops or supermarkets, but if you can get them, you can replace the damsons in the above recipe (but reduce the water to only one pint) and it will give you a jam that is softer and sweeter than an ordinary plum. If you have access to a copper jelly pan, you can end up with a beautiful pale green preserve that will impress your guests. English fruit is far more reliable than the imported variety and produces a brighter green jam!

GOOSEBERRY AND ELDERFLOWER

If you have ever read any historical novels where there has been a description of the food and its accompaniments that was being eaten during a meal, you will have heard of this one. Gooseberries are, to my mind, a much underrated fruit but with the combination of elderflowers which adds an extra dimension to this truly, beautiful jam; it is a most English fruit. It can be eaten either as a jam, with bread, or used as a tracklement with roast goose. Gooseberries tend to be an antidote to the extra fat that is part of the goose and our ancestors must have found that it was a good complement.

Elderflowers appear in late spring and the earlier that you collect them the better. If you leave collection after the flowers are passed their best then often the stock that you make from them will have an unpleasant edge to its taste. Some people say that the stock then smells of cats!
I, personally, do not like the subtle change in the smell, so I collect them soon after they open. Collect the flowers by cutting the heads and dropping these into a bag, try not to shake them as this will dislodge the pollen. 15 heads will make about a quart (two pints) of stock.
To make the stock, put the heads into a sauce pan. Cover them with water and quickly drain it off, then re-cover the heads with water and leave in a closed pan for a day or so. Pour the fluid through a fine strainer into a large container and leave to settle. Decant this fluid and use it to make your jam.
If you can make more than you need, the surplus can be frozen in plastic bottles.

GOOSEBERRY AND ELDERFLOWER

You will need

4½ lbs of gooseberries, which have been "topped and tailed"
1¾ pints of the decanted elderflower juice
4½ lbs of sugar

Method

Cook the gooseberries in the elderflower juice for about 15 minutes, in an aluminium pan.

Add the sugar and bring to the boil.

Initially boil the mixture gently to allow the deep pink colour to develop but towards the end of the cooking process, raise the temperature and boil until you get a good set.

Pour into clean dry jars and seal.

This will make about eight pounds of jam which if kept cool and dark will keep for well over a year. It does tend to get rather rubbery after a year but the taste is still there.

GOOSEBERRY AND MINT

This is another of those preserves that can either be used as a tracklement or as a jam. The choice is yours.

It is the Scots that know of this recipe more as a jam, whereas those from south of the border tend to raise their eyebrows at the combination. My aunt first introduced me to the flavours when she served some with mackerel that had been fried in oats. She did not live far from the fishing harbour and therefore knew when the fishing boats were due to come in. As kids, we were often sent down to the harbour to "catch" the fish which dropped off the boxes as they were swung over the side of the boat. The sport was to catch the fish before the gulls and then return home triumphant with our spoils.
Again the gooseberries complement the oily fish and the combination is delicious.

But I have been told that it is "excellent in ham sandwiches". That was a comment from someone over the shoulder of a customer! Try it for yourself and see if you agree.
I like it as a jam on brown toast. The choice is yours.

You will need

4½ lbs of gooseberries
4½ lbs of sugar
1½ pints of water
3 heaped dessert spoons of chopped mint,
or 3 teaspoons of bottled garden mint
A copper preserving pan

GOOSEBERRY AND MINT

Method

Cook the gooseberries in the water for about 15 minutes in the copper pan.

Add the sugar and boil quickly to get a good set. You have to work quickly or else you will lose the green colour of the gooseberries. It does not alter the flavour but as a green jam it is intriguing.
The sugar you use can be a mixture of half and half of granulated and pectin sugars, as this will give a quicker set.

When ready add the mint and return the mixture to boiling point.

Pour into clean jars and seal.

This will make seven to eight pounds of jam that will keep for well over a year.

HARLEQUIN!

I am always asked "Why, Harlequin?" It is a difficult question to answer unless you know that a Harlequin is a "joker" and that he is invariably dressed in both red and yellow.
The red and yellow could be thought of as the raspberries (or redcurrants) and the pineapple. But it is far more than that! Not quite a joke but certainly an enigmatic attack to the taste buds. A beautiful red jam and as such gives your mental taste buds the expectation of what red jam should taste like and in the initial taste it is just that but it has the over-ride of the taste of the oranges which says to your senses "this is not red jam". So it is this mixture of tastes that make it well deserving of its name.

You will need

1 lb of redcurrants
1 lb of raspberries
½ lb of prepared Seville oranges
Large can (430g or 12 ozs) of unsweetened crushed pineapple
Large can (430g or 12 ozs) of unsweetened black cherries
½ pint of water
4½ lbs of sugar *(I use half the quantity of pectin-added sugar and half ordinary sugar, as the cherries and pineapple contain no natural pectin.)*

HARLEQUIN!

Method

Cook the redcurrants, raspberries and oranges in the water for about 20 minutes.

Use this time to de-stone the cherries.

Add the pineapple and the cherries, along with the juices that they are in, and cook the whole mix together for a further 30 minutes.

Add the sugar and boil rapidly until you get a good set.

Pour into clean dry jars and seal immediately.

This will make about eight pounds of a beautiful jam that is delightful on plain scones.
It will keep for about a year but do keep it in a cool and dark place to help preserve the colour.

HALF SUGAR JAMS & MARMALADES

Theses recipes are suitable for anyone who is following a low sugar diet. These include many who are diabetics and especially those who control their condition by diet, although I do have some customers who are also insulin users.
Most jams can be adapted but I have found that one of the best is made by using blackcurrants with apple to assist the set.
I also do a strawberry and gooseberry jam, again with apple, and this is a pale jam but nevertheless tastes just as good. The general rule of thumb is to keep the water level to about half of that used in the normal jam and use half as much sugar as the fruit when put it in the pan!

You will need
1 lb of prepared apples, after peeling and coring
1 lb of blackcurrant's or 1 lb (each) of strawberries and gooseberries
1 lb or 1½ lbs of sugar (for the strawberry and gooseberry)
½ pint of water

Method

Put the apples with the water in a pan, with a lid, and cook until you can smash them to a purée. I use a potato masher for this purpose.
Add the rest of the fruit and cook it until all of the fruit is soft. You will need to keep the pan stirred or else the fruit will stick and burn. This process will take a further 15 minutes.

HALF SUGAR JAMS & MARMALADES

Method (*contd*)

Add the sugar and bring the mixture back to a brisk boil until you achieve a set. This will not be as hard a set as ordinary jams but do not overcook the mixture as this will spoil both the flavour and the colour.
When satisfied, pour the jam into clean dry jars and seal.

This will make about three to four pounds of jam, which will keep for about six to eight months, if kept cool and dark. It has a lower shelf-life than normal because the temperature reached before the setting point is achieved is lower than in ordinary jams.

HALF-SUGAR MARMALADE can be made in a similar way by using 1 lb of dessert oranges, with a lemon, ¾lb of prepared apples and one pound of sugar, in ¾ of a pint of water.
Cut up the oranges and lemons, then cook them in the water until the hulls are soft. This should take about 45 minutes.
Chop the apples and add them to the pan and cook again until the apples are soft after about 15 minutes.
Add the sugar and reheat the mixture to boil gently until you have a good set.
Pour the cooling mixture into clean dry jars and seal them. As with the jam, the marmalade has a limited shelf-life but is comparatively easy to make so make small batches of it.

MARMELO (OR QUINCE CHEESE)

This jam belongs in the primeval era of jam making. Historically, its use can be traced back to Roman times when the fruits of autumn were preserved in honey for winter use. Most fruits would lend themselves to being preserved cold but not the quince. These fruits needed cooking to soften them before the preservative properties of honey would have any affect and the cooking released the setting power of the pectin in the fruit making a very firm preserve. It was used as an after-dinner sweetmeat to combat the richness of their foods.
In more recent times, this jam has fallen out of favour and the fruit has been replaced by others. In the middle-ages, citrus fruit started to be used instead; nevertheless, if you can find some quince, or the fruit of the japonica, it is well worth the trouble of collecting them and making this uniquely different preserve.

Ask your gardening friends what they do with their fruits. If they will then give them to you, you can always repay them with a jar of the jam!

You will need

A good 2 pints of prepared Quince pulp, this requires about four or five lbs of quinces
2 large lemons
½ pint of water
4 lbs of sugar

MARMELO (OR QUINCE CHEESE)

Method

Wash the bloom off the quince and, using a sharp knife, cut them in half to ensure that there are no maggots or bugs lurking in the core of the fruit. If the fruits are large, cut them into small pieces, as they will cook better. Put the pieces of quince into a pan and cover them with water. Cook the fruit slowly for at least an hour until the fruits are mushy and are starting to turn red. If you can cover the pan during this time it will improve the flavours through the cooking of the fruit. Rub the "mush" through a wire sieve, discarding the residue of pips and skin. This is now your quince pulp and any extra that is not needed can be frozen and kept till the next time.

Cook the lemons in half a pint of water for about 35 minutes and when the hulls are soft, remove the pips and, in a food blender, homogenise the lemons and water juice mixture.

Measure two pints of the quince pulp and the homogenised lemon into an aluminium pan, add the sugar and bring the mixture to boiling point.

Simmer slowly. You will need to stir the mixture frequently at this stage to stop it sticking and also to allow the colour to develop. It will take 45 minutes (or longer) to turn to a rich red colour, then it should be ready to pot.

Test for a set, then pour into clean dry jars and seal immediately.

This will make about eight pounds of a deliciously different, sharp jam. You can also assure your guests that they are about to sample the Original Marmalade. This marmalade has a shelf life about a year.

JAMS

PLUM JAMS, "*WITH A DIFFERENCE*"

In this part of rural England, that is the county of Worcestershire, I always feel that Plum Jam is considered by the locals, to be a poor man's jam, simply because at the right time of the year there is an over abundance of plums and everyone, who can, will make the fruits into jam.
This bounty may be good for the store cupboard but not when I am persuading my customers that this jam is something different. So I set out to make it just that.
Over a period of time and after some experimentation, I decided on an additional ingredient that would turn an ordinary plum jam into something extra-ordinary.

Jam made with the early variety of black plums, known as Czar, gains from the addition of a little brandy.
Victoria plums are enhanced both in colour and flavour by the addition of a little port wine.
The yellow, Pershore egg plums are spectacularly spiced with peach Schnapps.

Each variety has their devotees amongst my customers and I offer the three favoured variations here.

You will need

4½ lbs of plums
4½ lbs of sugar
5 fl ozs of the "right" alcohol spirit
1 pint of water

PLUM JAMS, "*WITH A DIFFERENCE*"

Method

In each case, cook the plums in the water for about 20 minutes and allow the mixture to cool.
You should now be able to remove the stones from the fruit in the pan by hand but do take care that the mixture is not too hot before you start.
Add the sugar and bring the mixture to the boil and then boil rapidly until you get a good set.
Leave the jam to cool for 20 to 30 minutes*, stirring occasionally.
Add the chosen alcohol and stir it in quickly. Pour the jam into clean dry jars and seal quickly.

Either way, you will make about eight pounds of jam that has a shelf life of at least 9 months.

* *The length of time that the jam is left to cool is fairly elastic and will depend on the ambient temperature of your kitchen. If left for too short a time and therefore the jam will be still too hot, the alcohol will fizz off. If on the other hand, the mixture is left too long then you will shorten the shelf life of the jam.*

PINEAPPLE AND LEMON

When you sit down to breakfast, what do you put on your toast if you do not like marmalade?

The answer is very simply - jam. In my opinion, pineapple and lemon jam. This jam is both sharp and sweet but is not red! All the emotions of breakfast are properly satisfied. Pineapples, by the time they reach the shops in England, have lost some of their acidity but nevertheless if you can find large "sugar-pines" they are well worth the effort of preparing them.

Wash the pineapple well and twist out the leaves, cut the surface off, going round the pineapple, then cut off the base. It does not matter if you get all the brown bits away with the first cutting as by cutting a V-shaped wedge diagonally along the flesh you can cut them out in lines without wasting too much of the useful pineapple.

A large "sugar-pine" will yield about 2 lb of fruit.

You will need

To every 2 lbs of prepared pineapple allow:
2 large (or 3 small) lemons
1 pint of water
3 ¼ lbs of sugar

PINEAPPLE AND LEMON

Method

Cut the cleaned pineapple into vertical slices that are about one inch by a quarter inch thick. Cut these slices into quarter inch pieces. I use the “julienne” attachment on my food processor for this.

Mince the lemons. Again you can do this chopping using a food processor and by having pieces of fruit, it gives the jam a good texture.

Simmer the fruit in the water for about 45 minutes.
Add the sugar and simmer for a further 30 minutes.

Raise the temperature and boil the mixture rapidly for a further 5 minutes, by which time you should get a good set. If it does not, then bring the jam back to a quick boil for a further few minutes until you do.

When you are happy with your set pour into clean dry jars and seal immediately.

This will make about four pounds of jam but if you double up the quantities you may be able to keep it long enough to test the shelf life but I think about ten months is a conservative estimate.

RHUBARB (OR MARROW) AND GINGER

Both of these are very old fashioned recipes that came out of my grandmother's kitchen!
Once I was exhibiting at a local agricultural show and a gentleman bought a jar of this Rhubarb and Ginger jam from my stall. He had a large voice, which complemented his large frame, and after he had purchased the jam, he boomed, "I haven't had this since I was a boy. My grandmother used to make it for tea!."
He promptly opened the jar, stuck his finger into the jam, pulled out a chunk and promptly ate it. Then, addressing his wife, who was on the other side of the large marquee and some distance away, he shouted, "Look what I have found."
Over she came to my stall and he passed her the jar and she repeated the finger-in-finger-out routine. Needless to say by this time they had attracted a considerable audience. I could not have stage-managed such advertising any better.
I have told the tale many times and it always makes me smile.

But these are now jams of times past.

Rhubarb is the first fruit after winter and was often used in the past to augment diminishing jam stocks until the soft fruits became available.
Marrow, on the other hand, came from lean times when fruit was in short supply but everyone had an abundance of marrows.
Both are excellent jams even though their shelf life is relatively short and I usually reckon on about eight months, but then I have never managed to keep them any longer. They have been eaten well before the expected "best before" date.

RHUBARB (OR MARROW) AND GINGER

You will need
4½ lbs of Rhubarb (or Marrow, after peeling and de-seeding)
4 ozs of root ginger, freshly grated
2 dessert spoons of chopped crystallised ginger
2 bags of Jam sugar, that is, sugar containing pectin (about 4½ lbs will be needed)

Method

Cut the fruit into small chunks.
Put these in the jelly pan with both the gingers, and stir round to mix the ginger with the fruit.
Pour the sugar over the mixture to cover the fruit completely and leave it to stand overnight, if possible.

In the morning, bring the mixture slowly to the boil and cook it gently for about 30 minutes when the fruit should then be soft (or the marrow transparent, if you are using this).

Raise the temperature and boil rapidly for two or three minutes by which time you should get a good set.
Reduce the heat to the minimum once again while you are waiting to check your test.

When set, pour into clean dry jars and seal immediately. This will make about seven to eight pounds of a very piquant jam. It has a limited shelf life (about 8 months) and needs to be kept stored in a cool and dark place.

RHUBARB AND REDCURRANT CONSERVE

Strictly this is a conserve, as it is not as solid as a jam should be but, nevertheless, it is still a superb combination of flavours.

I always think that it combines the best from both fruits and is a very good "breakfast jam", as it has a sharpness that is a good wake up call to the taste buds. It is simply divine on fresh toast. I have tried making this by leaving the pips in the mixture but somehow this does not produce the quality of jam that I personally like to offer. You could try it but I would recommend that you follow my method.

You will need

2¼ lbs of Redcurrants
2¼ lbs of Rhubarb
4½ lbs of Sugar*
½ pint of water

* *Should the rhubarb be grown in an excessively wet season, you would be well advised to use half pectin sugar and half ordinary sugar, as this will give you a better set without overcooking your jam.*

RHUBARB AND REDCURRANT CONSERVE

Method

Cook the redcurrants in water for about 30 minutes.

Pour the whole contents of your pan into a metal sieve placed over a jelly pan.

Rub the fruit (now held in the sieve) with the back of a wooden spoon so that all of the flesh of the currants goes through into the juice in the pan whilst the pips are held in the sieve ready to be discarded. I repeat the rubbing until the residue looks dry. This way you are gaining most of the flesh off the redcurrants and leaving most of the pips in the sieve.

Chop the rhubarb into about half-inch lengths and add to the redcurrant stock in the jelly pan. Cook together until the rhubarb starts to break down, this will take about 30 minutes.

Add the sugar and bring the mixture to the boil, maintain at boiling point until you get a good set.

Pour into clean dry jars and seal immediately.

This will make seven to eight pounds of a deep red jam that will keep, if kept in a cool and dark place, for nine months or more. Try it as an alternative to marmalade!

STRAWBERRY IN COINTREAU

Inevitably when I attend a craft fair or exhibition I am asked, by some passer-by, "Ain't you got no strawberry jam?"
When I point out this particular jam, I invariably get the retort, "Just Strawberry, don't want anything else!"
I often feel like saying "If you want just strawberry jam go to the supermarket and buy some." It is there on the shelves of most grocers. A jar of honest, plain, ordinary strawberry jam.
I did have one comment which really made me laugh. It was made by a little old lady and delivered in a broad Black Country accent, when she pointed to the jar and turned to her friend and came out with the immortal comment, "Oo-o-oh look! It's got strawberries in it!" What else would you expect in a strawberry jam! We all laughed at what she said but she was so surprised to see the real fruits in the jar that it incurred that exclamation! Yes, it has got real strawberries in it and if you are careful you can produce a jam with whole fruits in a red jelly!
On a personal note, my grand-daughter will not go home after a visit to me without a jar of this jam, so it must be quite special for her.

You will need
4½ lbs of strawberries
2 x 1 kg bags of jam sugar (with pectin)
5 fl ozs of Cointreau

STRAWBERRY IN COINTREAU

Method

Crush the larger strawberries, for which I use a potato masher as my tool of choice, but keep the smaller fruits whole in an aluminium preserving pan.
Pour half of the sugar over the fruit and leave this, preferably overnight, so that the juices can leak out of the fruits and this will then provide some liquid in which to cook the fruit.
Bring the mixture to the boil and maintain this temperature for no more than 10 minutes so that the fruit will cook and soften, without breaking down. Add the remainder of the sugar and bring the mixture back to boiling point. Maintain this boil for five minutes keeping a fairly rapid boil through the jam during this time.
Take the pan off the heat and pour a small quantity onto a cold saucer to test for a set.*
Let the jam cool in the pan for about 30 minutes before adding the Cointreau. Stir the liquor into the mixture thoroughly.
Pour the resultant mixture into clean, dry jars and seal them quickly to preserve the kick of the Cointreau.

This will make about seven pounds of a most delicious jam. Store it in a cold and dark place, in effect hide it, as it will be eaten.
It has a shelf life of about 8 months.

** The set will produce a looser jam than many other recipes but it is worth maintaining the exquisite taste at the expense of a hard set.*

SUMMER FRUITS

I created this jam as I had a small amount of a variety of fruits, what I would call the soft fruits of summer, left over in my fridge. Fruits such as gooseberries, strawberries, raspberries and blackcurrants are the types I mean. Once I had some redcurrants left in the freezer and I had a plentiful supply of rhubarb. Except for the rhubarb, there was not enough of any other fruit to do anything with. What do you do?

On the adage that nothing ventured is nothing gained, I put them all in the pan, added an approximate equal amount of rhubarb and thought here goes. Go, it went on to produce a beautiful red jam. It looks right, tastes even better and has made a good talking point for those who have never made jam! The uninitiated invariably come up with the comment "How do you get all those fruits in one jar?"

I think that they must think that you, the cook, put the raw fruit in the jar and somehow by saying some magic words it turns miraculously into jam.

It is the combination, each fruit adding something, sweetness (strawberries), sharpness (rhubarb), setting (gooseberries), colour and strength (currants), that meld so well together.

An excellent jam particularly with scones and cream!

SUMMER FRUITS

You will need

A good pound, in weight, of each of the following fruits; strawberries, raspberries, blackcurrants, redcurrants, gooseberries and rhubarb. You do not have to be exact with the weight but avoid overloading the mix with any one particular fruit as this will tend to spoil the balance of flavours.

In total, you will need about 6 lbs of fruit
1 pint of water
6½ lbs of sugar

Method

Cook all the fruit in the water for about 20 minutes, until all of it is softened and the juice is a deep, rich red. Add the sugar and return the mixture to the boil, maintain this until you have a uniform colour, raise the temperature and boil rapidly for about 10 minutes. Test for a set.*
Pour into clean dry jars and seal.

This will make about twelve pounds of jam that will keep well if stored in a cool and dark place. It will keep for a year as long as you do not have many visitors to tea!

* *Turn the heat down or off while waiting for the 'test' to cool, as there always is a danger that it will either overcook or spoil the colour or stick!*

GENERAL NOTES FOR MAKING CHUTNEYS

What is “chutney”?
Chutney is a tangy, sweet pickle, thought to be of Indian origin, usually served as an accompaniment to curries, hot and cold meats, chesses and savouries. There are many varieties but all are based on a mixture of chopped fruit and vegetables, sugar and vinegar.

- Assemble all you ingredients before you start.
- Grind any spices in a pestle and mortar. There is little need to have a dust fine mixture as often the bits will add to the texture.
- Remember that you can always add more spice but you cannot take it out, that particularly applies to the hot spices such as chillies.
- I prefer to use white spiced vinegar, but the malt vinegars can also be used in darker chutney. Occasionally if I want something extra-special I will use a Wine or Cider Vinegar.
- In general, do not be in too much of a hurry; maintain the pan at boiling point but do not overheat. Time allows the mixture to meld.
- The exceptions to this rule of thumb is where you add nuts and want to keep the crunch, or if you add dates, where you want to keep them distinct from the rest of the mixture, then add these just before you bring the mixture to the final boiling point.

GENERAL NOTES FOR MAKING CHUTNEYS

- Because of the nature of the mixture, almost all chutneys have a tendency to stick to the pan and thus need continual monitoring and/or stirring.
- Too much of any one taste can ruin a good balance. Write down what you put in so that you can replicate what is good and avoid what is not.
- Until you find what you like, do not make tons of the stuff. When you find a good one then make it in quantity and store the extra. Become a squirrel!
- Give your surplus as presents to friends. Find me the poor spirit that is not delighted with such a gift!
- Use an aluminium pan, the vinegar will often spoil stainless steel and it attacks copper. If you can keep a pan just for Chutneys then you will not need to worry if the smell of vinegar sticks.
- If you can, have a pan with a lid. This stops the liquid boiling off and makes for a better-balanced mixture in the end.
- Remember most chutneys improve for keeping; the more mixed the fruits or vegetables, and the more ginger there is in the recipe, the general rule of thumb is to keep it for a month and then "enjoy".

ASPARAGUS RELISH

This is a recipe that was created when I was offered some asparagus which was all bent and in a sad state and frankly not suitable for selling to the discerning public who like their "grass" in the round, with all the stalks straight and of uniform size and thickness.
Well natural things don't grow like that! Therefore, I was asked if I could create chutney from it, as there was not one available on the English market.
I thrive on challenges like that and spent a few happy hours thinking before I tried to create the recipe given below which is the result of my deliberations. For me asparagus has to be creamy but not lose its texture. The "grass" is made of two different parts; the stalk and the head, so it needs two different processes. Try it and see how you get on. You will not be disappointed.
This will make an excellent accompaniment to poached salmon or ham.

CHUTNEYS

You will need

2½ lbs of asparagus,
¼ lb of butter
2 medium eggs
6 fl ozs of white wine vinegar
1 pint of water
½ lb of white sugar
1 tablespoon of cornflour

Spices –
½ teaspoon of each of the following:-
freshly ground white pepper, salt, powdered mustard or mustard seeds, chilli seeds or a finely chopped green chilli, pickling spice and pimento.

ASPARAGUS RELISH

Method

Prepare the asparagus by cutting off the heads and putting them in a separate bowl. Wash the remaining stalks and cut them into small (¼ inch) slices. Put these in a covered pan with about half a pint of the water and steam gently for about 45 minutes.
Put the contents of the pan into a liquidiser or food processor and homogenise the stalks.
Break the eggs into this mixture while the machine is running. Transfer the contents of the liquidiser to an aluminium pan together with all the spices, the vinegar and the butter. Bring gently to the boil.
Meanwhile wash and chop the heads of the asparagus into the same sized pieces, (the smaller the pieces, the finer will be the texture of the finished relish but the quicker it will cook).
Add the chopped heads to the now simmering mixture and maintain the temperature for about five minutes. Keep it stirred or it will stick to the bottom of the pan. Add the sugar and cook gently for a further five to ten minutes.
Mix the cornflour with the remaining water and add to the pan. Keep it stirred and bring the mixture back to a gentle boil for another five minutes when you should have a pale green mixture with dark green bits.
Carefully ladle it into clean, dry jars and seal. It will be ready to eat in about a week.
This will make about five pounds of relish, which will need to be kept cold (refrigerated) and should then keep for about six to eight months, if you do not eat it all first!

BANANA CHUTNEY

Whenever I can find some large "fit" bananas, at a decent price, I will make this one. It is an excellent compliment to curries and with any foods where you want a soft chutney.

Oftentimes, at the market, on a Saturday afternoon, just before the close of trading, traders are very willing to sell off their bananas and I am very willing to buy. This chutney comes from an idea that I created in the West Indies when I was trying to generate a banana jam.

No luck there but this is a very good alternative and easy to make.

You will need

5 or 6 large bananas, that are not over-ripe
1 lb of cooking apples
¼ lb of onions
6 ozs of raisins
¼ teaspoon of salt
¼ teaspoon of cayenne pepper
2 good teaspoons of ground ginger
½ pint of white spiced vinegar
½ lb of light brown sugar

BANANA CHUTNEY

Method

Prepare the apples and chop the onions finely, put these in an aluminium pan with the vinegar and cook until the apples are light and fluffy. This will take about 30 minutes Mash them through with a potato masher.
Add the salt, pepper, ginger and raisins and cook for a further 10 minutes. This allows time for the raisins to swell.
Mash, or chop, the bananas and add these to the pan with the sugar; stir the mixture well and continue stirring until it is back to boiling point. Maintain this for about 30 minutes, stirring frequently or the chutney will stick.

Your chutney should now be thick and quite pale. If you want a darker chutney, cook it for longer, but be careful to keep it stirred or it will stick.

Spoon the mixture into clean dry jars working it down, with a spoon, to leave no air pockets then seal the jars and store them in a cool dark place.
This recipe should make between four and five pounds of chutney that is ready to eat straight away but will keep for a year.

It is good chutney to eat with strong spicy foods, as it will ameliorate the spice and add its own smoothness.

BEETROOT CHUTNEY

I do not claim this as an original recipe but I add it to this collection as I have found that it is a very popular chutney. It is "ordinary" and yet it is an excellent complement to cold meats. Folk always want a type of chutney to eat with anything, but I do feel that certain varieties are good with certain foods and not so good with others. Perhaps you will disagree but then it would not do for us all to think alike. Nevertheless, try this with cold pork and a salad ... it is good! Enjoy both the taste and the colour!

You will need

3½ lbs of beetroot
1 lb of prepared apples
1 lb of onions
8 ozs of sultanas
1 lb of white sugar
1¼ pints of white, spiced vinegar
½ teaspoon of salt

Method

Cook the beetroot for about 45 minutes and leave to cool. Make sure that they do not boil dry at any stage of the cooking*.
Finely chop the onions and the apples and cook them in the vinegar, preferably in a covered pan.
Skin the beetroot** and chop it finely and add to the apples and onions, add the salt and cook altogether for about 30 minutes.

BEETROOT CHUTNEY

Method (contd)

Use a food processor to do the chopping as it makes for a nice, fine chutney. You will have to stir the mixture frequently to stop it sticking to the pan.
Add the sultanas and maintain at boiling point for a further 10 minutes to swell them. Add the sugar and bring back to the boil. Maintain it at this temperature for a further 15 minutes to meld the sugar with the 'fruits'.
Carefully ladle into clean dry jars and seal.

This will make about eight pounds of a delightfully simple but beautiful chutney that will grace any plate.

It can be eaten straight away ... let it cool first ... but it will happily keep for a twelve months or more, so make enough in the autumn to last you through until the next crop of roots are ready for harvesting. To maintain the colour, keep it in a cool and dark cupboard or storeroom.

** I was taught a method to ensure that the beetroot does not bleed, and so I cut the stalks off about an inch above the bulb, and then keep them covered whilst cooking. I allow the globes to cool in the water in which they have been cooked. I usually try to cook them the day before so that I do not have to wait for them to cool.*

*** No matter how hard I try I cannot avoid getting everything coloured a deep red, so be careful not to get splashes on to clothing. A good tip is to use latex rubber gloves when skinning the roots; that way you do not end up with red stained hands!*

CARROT AND CORIANDER CHUTNEY

This beautiful chutney will grace any table just by its colour. It has the disadvantage that you can not eat it straight away but it requires about a month to really meld the flavours together and produce a good complement, particularly to cold meats. Folk are always attracted by the name and I usually get the comment, "Well, I like the soup, so I am sure that I will like that." but to me it is the added crunch of the almonds that really make it different to other chutneys.

You will need

2½ lbs of carrots, grated
2 large lemons, chopped in a food processor
4 ozs of root ginger, grated or chopped in a food processor
½ pint of white vinegar, (wine vinegar is best but spiced vinegar runs a close second)
½ pint of water
3 tablespoons of golden syrup
3 teaspoons of coriander seeds, ground in a pestle and mortar
½ teaspoon of dried chilli seeds
1 teaspoon of salt
¾ lb of light brown or white sugar
3 good tablespoons of flaked almonds

CARROT AND CORIANDER CHUTNEY

Method

Put the lemons and ginger in an aluminium pan with the water and cook slowly for about 15 minutes.

Add all the remaining ingredients, except the sugar and almonds to the pan, stir thoroughly and bring to boiling point, cover the pan and maintain the temperature for a further 45 minutes to allow the carrots and lemon hulls to become soft. You will have to stir the mixture periodically to stop it sticking to the pan but try not to allow too much evaporation of the liquid. (If it becomes dry, add a little water as this will ensure a soft texture to the fruit).

Add the sugar, return to simmer point and maintain this for a further 30 minutes, keep the mixture stirred and the pan covered, if possible.
Add the almonds and stir in, bringing the contents of the pan back to boiling point.
Spoon the mixture into clean dry jars and seal.

This will make about six pounds of chutney, which needs to be left for about a month to develop. It will keep for well over a year if kept cold and dark.

DATE AND ORANGE CHUTNEY

This recipe was one of those that I started with a name and then I set about creating an acceptable taste that fits the concept.
I had acquired a bag of oranges that were almost too good to be true in their colour and the combination of orange and brown was very fashionable at the time. My thinking was to create a fashionable chutney using suitable spices that were the right colour and would complement the taste of the very fruity oranges. It is a brilliant complement to cheeses like Red Leicester but eats well with Cheddar and any of the hard cheeses.

You will need

2 lbs of dessert oranges, the brighter the better, minced or chopped
2 lbs of prepared cooking apples
8 ozs of onions, chopped finely
8 ozs of dates (after stoning) chopped into three
1 pint of spiced white vinegar
1 lb of light brown or white sugar

Spices
1 tsp of powdered mustard
1 tsp of ground ginger
½ tsp of white pepper
½ tsp of mixed spice
¼ tsp of tumeric or saffron
¼ tsp of schaschlick spice
½ tsp of salt (optional)

DATE AND ORANGE CHUTNEY

Method

When you have prepared the fruit, put the oranges, apples and onions with the spices in an aluminium pan with the vinegar, bring this mixture to the boil and maintain it at the boiling point for about 45 minutes, or until the orange peel has softened.

Add the sugar and bring the mixture back to boiling point. Stir it occasionally or it will stick to the bottom of the pan; keep it at boiling point for a further 30 minutes. When the mixture has thickened and the individual fruits are no longer distinguishable, add the chopped dates. Try not to break down the texture of the dates as you stir them in.

Make sure that the mixture has re-boiled after the addition of the dates.

Ladle into clean dry jars, seal as quickly as you can preferably with a lid that will produce a good airtight seal. Store the jars in a cool dark place.

This will make about eight pounds of chutney, which has the advantage that it can be eaten as soon as it cools. It has a shelf life of a year or more if stored correctly.

Keep it cool and dark to maintain the colour.

FRUIT TRILOGY CHUTNEY

I developed the idea for this chutney, made with three fruits that I would not have thought of putting together except for the fact that there was a possibility of using the colour change that occurs with gooseberries and apples to produce a pink chutney. It takes time and needs patience but I think that it is worthwhile as it does make a good-looking complement to pale cheeses. It is one of my favourites and could become one of yours if you like fruity chutney.

You will need

1 lb of gooseberries,
1¼ lbs of Victoria plums
1¼ lbs of apples
10 ozs of onions
6 ozs of raisins
1½ lbs of sugar
½ pint of water
½ pint of white vinegar
½ teaspoon of freshly ground red peppercorns
½ teaspoon of pickling spice
½ teaspoon of cinnamon
1 teaspoon of ginger

FRUIT TRILOGY CHUTNEY

Method

Cook the gooseberries in the water (in an aluminium pan).
Add 1 lb of the sugar and bring back to the boil, maintain the temperature, stirring occasionally until the mixture turns red. This will take about 45 minutes and is worth allowing the time to achieve a good colour in the final chutney.

Meanwhile stone the plums and peel the onions and apples.

Chop the onions and cook them in the vinegar until they are transparent.
Add the apples, chopped small, to the onions and cook for about 5 minutes, until fluffy. Add the raisins and allow them to swell.
Add the plums (chopped) and the gooseberry mixture, stir all together and bring back to the boil. Add the remaining sugar and the spices. Bring back to boiling and maintain this temperature for a further 20 minutes. Ladle into clean dry jars and seal.

This will make about six pounds of a very good-looking chutney. Il would suggest keeping it for a month before eating it although it will keep for a year or more, if you do not eat it in the meantime.

GRANNY T'S CHUTNEY

Folk always ask me what this is and I explain that it is a very traditional apple chutney; for the recipe must be about 150 years old. Invariably the riposte that I get from my customers is to ask why it is called Granny T's and I explain.

In our local craft group, we have a lady who is a wood turner and it is her granny's recipe. I never knew her granny but I have immortalised her by naming this recipe after her so it is "Granny T's". Sue, the wood turner, is a 'Tincello' so what better title. It has a nice ring and ably suits this particular chutney.

You will need:-

3 lbs of prepared, and chopped, cooking apples
1 lb of onions, chopped small
¾ pint of spiced malt vinegar
½ lb of sultanas
1 lb of Demerara sugar
½ teaspoon of salt
½ teaspoon of cayenne pepper (or ¾ tsp, if you want a more spikey chutney)

GRANNY T'S CHUTNEY

Method

Put the onions and the vinegar in a large aluminium pan and cook gently until the onions are transparent.
Add all the other ingredients, except the sugar, and cook for a further 30 minutes.
Add the sugar, stir it well and boil for a further 20 minutes.
Ladle into clean dry jars and seal when cool.

This will make about seven pounds of chutney that is delicious either with cold meats or with cheese.

I will often use Muscavado sugar as it gives a very rich dark colour but it is not as sweet as when you use Demerara .

To make a **MINTED APPLE CHUTNEY**, use white vinegar, white sugar and 2 teaspoonfuls of ground ginger (in place of the cayenne).
Just before the chutney is ready, add 3-4 tablespoons of chopped fresh mint or 3-4 teaspoons of bottled mint.

Do not let it overcook, and you will be rewarded with a pretty, green chutney that looks as good as it tastes.
This makes a very good complement to cold pork or lamb.
Personally, I like it with curry!

"HOT" TOMATO CHUTNEY

This was one of the first chutneys that I ever made and it has proved very popular with my customers. I probably make more of this chutney than I do of any other. Whether it is the colour or the suggestion that it is "hot", I do not know. It is very good, particularly with cheese.
If you are making it for yourself, you might like to increase the quantity of chillies that you put in but I always advise folk to add a little at a time, you can always add more but you cannot take it out once it is in the pan. I like a spicy chutney but I do not like to lose the taste of the fruits due to the overriding taste of the chilli. So take care, put a little of the chutney on a spoon and leave it to cool, then taste it, and then if you want it hotter you can add a little more chilli before bottling the chutney.

You will need

2 lbs 10 ozs of red tomatoes
2 lbs 10 ozs of cooking apples
2 lbs of onions
2 lbs of sultanas
2 lbs of light brown sugar
2 pints of spiced vinegar (preferably, white)

Spices
1 rounded teaspoon of hot chilli powder
½ to 1 rounded teaspoon of crushed chillies
1 teaspoon of salt
1 teaspoon of cayenne pepper
25 cloves, ground in a pestle and mortar

"HOT" TOMATO CHUTNEY

Method

Skin the tomatoes by dropping them into a bowl of boiling water*. Chop the onions as small as you can; coarsely chop the apples and tomatoes and put all these with the vinegar, in an aluminium pan, together with the salt and spices. Bring to the boil and simmer for about 30 minutes. By this time, the fruits should be soft and beginning to break down. Add the sultanas and cook slowly for a further 30 minutes. Add the sugar then bring the mixture back to boiling point and maintain it at this temperature for a further 2 hours.

Occasionally stir the chutney during this time to stop it sticking but also to keep track on how the colour is developing. It will change from a pale mixture to a rich red-brown and the longer it is cooked the better is the colour.

When the chutney has achieved the correct colour and is ready, ladle the mixture into clean dry jars and seal with an airtight lid.

It will make about thirteen pounds of chutney that can be eaten straight away but does improve for keeping. It will keep for well over a year.

In addition, because it takes so long to cook and to develop the colour, it is difficult to make it in small quantities, so make this amount and give some to friends. They will welcome the gift! However, it is worth making the extra as you will make friends when they have tasted it.

** Tip - I prefer to freeze the tomatoes first as the skins are then easily removed when they are dropped into the water.*

LIME PICKLE

When you get lime pickle at a restaurant, does it really taste of limes?
I have tried several and every time I have ended up with a burning sensation in my mouth that removes the ability to taste anything. Limes are very special in that they are very full of flavour and are a deep green but therein lies the problem. If you want to retain the green colour, you should not cook them in an aluminium pan, conversely if you want to make a pickle you should use an aluminium pan.
Therefore, the dilemma that I was faced with when I was asked to make a lime pickle was how to make it taste just right every time. I reasoned that courgettes would keep their colour, but not mask the taste of the limes. Apple would add to the texture and onions would give flavour. Add in a combination of spices and the result given here was achieved. A pickle, with a variety of flavours, and you can taste the limes.
Try it with cold meats, particularly chicken or ham.

You will need-

6 good sized limes, these should weigh about 1 lb
Equal weights of prepared apples, onions and courgettes (making 4 lb altogether)
6 ozs of sultanas
7 fl ozs of water
14 fl ozs of white spiced vinegar
1½ lbs of white sugar

Spices
1½ tsp of ground ginger
½ tsp of ground coriander
¼ tsp of ground cumin
¾ tsp of white pepper
¾ tsp of paprika
¼ tsp of salt

LIME PICKLE

Method

Prepare and chop the onions and apples.
Cut the limes in half lengthwise and then in three, slicing as thinly as possible.
I will often put them in my food processor and chop them small as this is easier and it does not detract from the finished pickle. Put these three ingredients in an aluminium pan with the water and the vinegar and bring to the boil, keep at boiling point for about 20 minutes adding a little more water if necessary.
Cut the courgettes in four, lengthwise, then slice thinly and add to the pan along with the spices etc. and cook gently for a further 20 minutes or until the lime hulls are softened.
Add the sultanas and cook for a further 10 minutes.
Add the sugar, bring back to boiling point and maintain this for a further 30 minutes.
(Keep the pickle stirred or it will stick to the bottom of the pan)
Ladle into clean dry jars and seal.

It will make about six pounds of a pickle that may be eaten within a week or so, but will keep for up to a year if stored in a cool dark place.

This will complement many Chinese and Indian dishes where you are looking for a full taste that is different to the bland rice and poppadums.

NICE AND SPICE CHUTNEY

I am always asked where do I get my ideas from?
A colleague had been having some work done on his house and one of the workmen had brought him a large bag of yellow Pershore plums. "Can your wife do something with these?" asked the workman. "No" said Brian, "but I know someone who can." and he brought them to me.
A large bag of rather over-ripe plums was waiting by my car. I had just made a batch of jam recently, so I decided to use the plums to make some chutney. After all chutneys take a lot of fruit which can be used when over-ripe!
Out came the stones and in went a selection of "sweet" spices, a little at a time, until I had a complementary taste to that which I had started with. It was fun, adding and tasting until I decided I had something really nice and spicy ....hence the name.

You will need

12 ozs of finely chopped onions
6 lbs of yellow egg plums, 12 fl ozs of white vinegar
6 ozs of sultanas
3 lbs of sugar
1 oz of rice flour, if required as a thickener

Spices
1 level teaspoon of each of the following,
Caraway, Nutmeg, Pimento, Cinnamon
Paprika, Allspice, White pepper
¼ teaspoon of ground cloves
3 rounded teaspoons of ground ginger
3 teaspoons of bottled mint or a good tablespoon of chopped fresh mint

NICE AND SPICE CHUTNEY

Method

Cook the onions in the vinegar in an aluminium pan until they are transparent, add the stoned plums and spices and boil until the plums are soft.*
Add the sultanas and bring back to the boil for about 10 minutes, add the sugar and again bring back to boiling point for a further 20 minutes, keep the chutney stirred so that it does not stick to the bottom of the pan.

If you want a thicker chutney, mix the rice flour with a little vinegar and add this mixture to the pan; stir well and maintain the temperature for an extra 10 minutes. Add the mint just before the chutney is ready to bottle (but make sure it has boiled through after the mint is added), pour into clean dry jars and seal with an airtight lid.

This will make about eight pounds of chutney. It will keep for twelve months if you store it in a cool dark place but I like to eat it so I can never keep it very long. It is brilliant with cheddar cheese and new bread... a real treat.

** An alternative to stoning the plums is to add them whole and, at this point, leave the pan and its contents to cool when you can then remove the stones by hand. I find this easier, particularly if the plums are frozen, but it does take longer.*

PEAR AND GINGER CHUTNEY

I am always being asked which is my personal favourite of the chutneys that I make. Undoubtedly, this is the one. For sheer taste and piquancy, this chutney will take a lot of beating. I liked the sound of the name and then set about trying to create something that would live up to the impression given by its title. I hope that I have achieved just that! You can try it and judge the result for yourself.
I am always delighted when folk come back for more of this chutney but more so when they do so with a comment that I can offer to future customers. One such comment came from a lady, by the name of Ann, who wanted it in large quantities as it was "so good with chicken, both hot and cold!" I personally like to eat it with soft cheese but do try it either way it is equally good!

You will need

2 lbs of pears (conference pears are best, but any pears will do)
1¼ lbs of prepared apples
2 small lemons
6 ozs of root ginger
6 ozs of onions
¼ teaspoon of salt
¼ teaspoon of ground white pepper
2 lbs of white sugar
¾ of a pint of white vinegar

PEAR AND GINGER CHUTNEY

Method

Cut the lemons in half, so that you can remove the pips.
Chop the lemons finely.
Chop the onions finely. I use a food processor for both.
Grate the ginger.

Put these ingredients in an aluminium pan with the vinegar, salt and pepper and bring this mixture to the boil, maintain the temperature for about 25 minutes.

While these are cooking, peel and chop, into small pieces, both the apples and the pears and then add to the pan. Cook for a further 20 minutes or until the apples have gone fluffy and the lemon peel is soft.

Add the sugar, bring back to the boil and maintain the temperature for a further 20 minutes, to meld the flavours, you will need to stir the mixture repeatedly to stop it sticking and burning.
Ladle into clean dry jars and seal immediately.

This recipe will make about six to seven pounds of chutney that will have a shelf life of a year. It does improve for keeping, so it is almost worth doubling up the quantities and hiding the second batch away in the store cupboard ... and not telling anyone where it is hidden!

PEACH CHUTNEY

I usually think of peaches as a luxury fruit that are far too nice to even think about cooking, never mind about turning into chutney. However and occasionally, if I am by the market late on a Saturday afternoon, the market stallholders are very willing to sell off their peaches at a reduced price, as the fruit will not keep until Monday! That is when I dive in and buy a load. Often at half price or less and usually, if I am lucky, they are ripe enough for turning into chutney. However if peaches are not available, this recipe will work, equally well, with Victoria plums. It is not quite so exotic in taste but is equally fruity.
I would recommend either.

You will need

4 lbs of peaches (or plums) stoned and chopped into small pieces
1 lb of onions, chopped finely*
1 pint of white spiced vinegar
4 ozs of raisins
2 lbs of white sugar
1 oz of rice flour, if it is required

Spices

2 rounded teaspoons of ground ginger
1 teaspoon of allspice
1 teaspoon of pickling spice, coarsely ground in a pestle and mortar

** A gentler chutney can be made by using red onions instead.*

PEACH CHUTNEY

Method

Put the onions with the ground spices in an aluminium pan with three quarters of the vinegar and cook until the onions become transparent.

You can be cutting the peaches while they are cooking. Add the chopped peaches and gradually bring back to the boil, maintain a gentle simmer for about 30 minutes, add the raisins and again maintain it at a gentle simmer for 15 minutes.

By this time the peaches will be cooked and the raisins swollen but all still distinct. Add the sugar and gently simmer for a further hour, stirring occasionally to prevent the chutney sticking.

If you like a thick chutney, mix the rice flour in the remainder of the vinegar and stir this into this mixture, otherwise add the remaining vinegar a little at a time to keep the level of liquid sufficient to enable the chutney to bubble. Cook for a further 15 minutes, ladle into clean dry jars and seal with a well fitting lid.

This chutney will improve if it is kept for a few weeks before it is eaten as this allows the spices to work through the fruits. This makes about six pounds of an excellent chutney that is delicious with cheeses such as Stilton or Wensleydale.

POACHER'S PICKLE

This is a pickle where the name has intrigued me for years, but I never had got around to thinking about what might go into such a pickle.

Obviously, it had to be something that was essentially rough so that the fruits would keep their individuality. I also felt that it had to be quite dominant in colour as well as taste, so I played around one morning and came up with this concoction, which I think will live up to its name as it will go with quite a selection of strong flavoured meats as well as cheeses.

You will need

½ lb of sun dried tomatoes
1 large red pepper, remove all the seeds first
¾ lb of onions
1 lb of prepared apples
1 pint of spiced vinegar
1 tsp of pickling spice freshly ground
½ teaspoon of salt
½ teaspoon of black pepper
6 ozs of raisins
1 lb of sugar

POACHER'S PICKLE

Method

Put the tomatoes, chopped onions salt and spices in an aluminium pan with the vinegar and cook gently for about 30 minutes.
Meanwhile chop the apples small and add these to the mixture in the pan, bring it back to the boil and maintain the temperature for about 10 minutes.

Chop the pepper into small pieces and add this to the mixture in the pan, together with the raisins, and keep the mixture at boiling point for a further 10 minutes. Keep it stirred or it will stick to the bottom of the pan.
Add the sugar; raise the temperature, keeping the mixture stirred for a further 45 minutes.

Carefully ladle the pickle into clean, dry jars and store somewhere cool and dark. This will make about five pounds of a beautifully dark pickle that can be eaten within a week, but it will improve for keeping.

It will have a shelf life of well over a year if it is not eaten in the meantime.

I would recommend making a double quantity and keep the second half hidden away from the kitchen gannets.

PUMPKIN AND PEPPER PICKLE

This recipe came into being as I liked the alliterative sound of the name and then I tried to create a pickle that would live up to the name. It always attracts attention as folk try to get their tongues round the twister. It is, therefore, a good talking point.
As always, having created something from a name, I then had to decide what it will complement.

It did not take me too long to decide on this one as it proved to be a brilliant complement to cold beef. Any meat where you want something to liven up the taste buds will be a reason for opening a jar of this pickle. I like the colour, as pumpkin makes a yellow "mush" and then the peppers make it interesting to look at; after that it is up to the taste buds to appreciate the combination.

You will need
2 lbs of diced pumpkin
¾ pint of white spiced vinegar
1 teaspoon of salt
2 teaspoons each of ground ginger, dry mustard and curry powder
¼ teaspoon of ground black pepper
½ lb of white sugar
½ red and ½ green peppers, cut into small cubes

PUMPKIN AND PEPPER PICKLE

Method

Put all ingredients, apart from the sugar and peppers, in an aluminium par, preferably one with a lid, and cook slowly for about 45 minutes.

Add the sugar and bring back to boiling point.
Simmer for a further 45 minutes, by which time the pumpkin should be soft and "squashable".

Add the diced peppers and bring the mixture back to boiling point for a further five minutes to "cook" the peppers, but do not overcook the mixture as you will lose the colour and so spoil the look of your finished pickle.

Ladle the mixture into clean dry jars, seal them and store them in a cool dark place.

This will make about three pounds of pickle that will keep for about a year but it will lose some of its colour. Because of the colour factor, I would advise making this pickle little and often rather than a big batch.

Tip
I keep the pumpkin, cut it into large chunks and bagged, in the freezer. The pumpkin will keep its colour until you need it.

RABBIE'S CHUTNEY

CHUTNEYS

Or **DATE AND WALNUT** *chutney, if you do prefer an alternative name for this chutney. I decided on the name due to a strange coincidence that happened at a Craft Fair that I attended.*
Talking to a customer about this chutney, which he assures me is "very good with Stilton Cheese", we found that we both came from the same part of Scotland as Robert Burns and were talking about him, when a lady, whilst looking at my stall, suddenly quoted from the Bard. A strange coincidence that three strangers should come together in rural Gloucestershire; all with a love of Burns, so I felt that it was auspicious to give it an appropriate name.

The challenge was to make a chutney that would fit "Date and Walnut" with no more information than that, so I have tried, and as a result I have produced a nice, sweet and crunchy chutney with enough "spike" for it to work with Stilton and yet not obscure the taste of the dates.

You will need

2 lbs of prepared cooking apples,
½ lb white sugar
½ lb of onions chopped small
1 - 1½ pints of white vinegar
¾ lb dates (each chopped in three pieces)
¼ lb of chopped walnuts (you can use pickled walnuts if you want a softer texture)

Spices
½ tsp of both pickling spices and Allspice, with eight cloves, ground in a mortar and pestle
¼ teaspoonful of cinnamon

RABBIE'S CHUTNEY

You will need (contd)
¼ teaspoon of salt
½ teaspoon of white pepper
½ teaspoon of ground ginger
1 tablespoonful of crystallised ginger, chopped into small pieces

Method

Cook the onions in 1 pint of vinegar in an aluminium pan.
Add the apples and cook them until they are light and fluffy.
Prepare and add all the spices to the pan and cook together for about 15 minutes.
Add the chopped dates and keep the mixture at boiling point, but be careful that it does not stick as time is needed for the dates to be incorporated into the mixture. Add the sugar and stir the mixture well.
Add more vinegar if the mixture gets too thick and dry looking. This process will take about half an hour.
Add the walnuts and bring the mixture back to boiling point for about five minutes.
Pack into jars and seal, quickly.

This will make about five pound jars of a chutney that will need time for the flavours to meld through and mature. It should be ready within a month and will keep for a year in a cool, dark place.

REAL ALE CHUTNEY

This is one that is rather unusual insomuch as it does not contain any onions neither does it contain any apples - both of which help to make the texture of the conventional chutney.
This chutney is a bit of a fiddle to make, particularly to get it into the jars after cooking.
It is well worth the bother and makes a good complement to cold meats, particularly beef or lamb.
Care in the preparation of the vegetables will make for an interesting texture.
I do not know whether it is the name but men, in particular, seem to hone in on it and I find it sells very quickly to them.
I always promise myself that I will make double the quantity but never manage to do so.

You will need

1 lb each of carrots, swede and cauliflower
½ lb of turnips
A can of ale, either ¾ of a pint or 440ml one, or an equivalent volume of draught ale
¾ pint of spiced malted vinegar
¾ lb of Demerara sugar
¼ lb of dates

Spices
1 teaspoon of salt
1½ teaspoon of ground ginger
A good ¼ teaspoon each of black pepper, cinnamon and mustard
Scant ¼ teaspoon of cumin

REAL ALE CHUTNEY

Method

Separate the cauliflower florets into very small pieces. Chop the swede, turnips and the stalks of the cauliflower using a fine food mincer, or food processor. Grate the carrots and put all these ingredients into an aluminium pan with the ale, vinegar and spices.
Bring to the boil and maintain it at a simmer point for about 45 minutes. Bring it back to the boil and add the sugar.
Keep the chutney stirred and just at boiling point for a further 30 minutes, making sure that you do not lose too much of the liquid or your chutney will be dry.
Meanwhile cut the dates into three and add these chunks to the mixture. Cook for a further five minutes.
Spoon the mixture through the liquid* and pack into clean dry jars.
This will make about seven pounds of chutney that will improve for keeping and has a shelf life of over a year.
Store in a cool dark place.
If you can acquire an ounce of horseradish root, this will make a very good addition to the chutney, especially if it is minced as with the other roots vegetables. You can use creamed horseradish instead, about three teaspoonfuls is needed, but too much will spoil the blend of flavours. So take care!

** Use a spoon that will fit into the neck of your jars so that when the chutney is transferred from pan to jar an equal amount of liquid is added to each jar. This liquid tends to be absorbed by the vegetables as the chutney is stored, and this makes for a good flavour when eventually the chutney is put out for eating.*

RED WINE CHUTNEY

When I was teaching, a colleague once organised a French evening and I was asked if I could make a chutney that would complement the various cheeses and breads that were going to be on offer. I made enquiries but was told by a fellow teacher, who taught French, that they, the French, do not eat sweet with sour. I was, therefore, on my own and thus had the challenge of producing something that might be thought of as remotely authentic. Wine and onions seemed to be the common denominators of all the suggestions that were made, so I have wound my way round them and created an intriguingly different chutney. Try it and see if you like it too. It is sweet and full of texture, so I see it as being a good complement to the soft cheeses like Brie.

You will need

2¼ lbs of red onions
2¼ lbs of cooking apples (peeled, cored and cut into quarters)
10 ozs of red cabbage
2¼ lbs of white sugar
5 ozs of raisins
1 level teaspoon of caraway seeds
½ teaspoon of white pepper
½ teaspoon of chilli seeds
A crushed clove of garlic
½ teaspoon of salt
1 pint of red wine vinegar
1 pint of red wine

RED WINE CHUTNEY

Method

Slice the apples and cook them in the vinegar until they are fluffy. Use an aluminium pan.
Prepare and chop both the onions and the cabbage and add these to the pan along with the remaining ingredients, except the sugar, raisins and the wine.
Cook very gently, stirring repeatedly until the cabbage has softened. This will probably take about an hour.
Add the raisins and leave these to cook for about half an hour for them to swell.
Add the sugar and wine and bring the mixture back to boiling point for a further 45 minutes.
If you can keep the pan covered during this time it will stop the wine boiling off, but keep the chutney stirred or it will stick to the pan.
When the whole mixture is melded together, ladle it into clean dry jars and seal as soon as possible.

This will make about eight pounds of a beautiful rich chutney. Its colour is a great complement to the creamy cheeses, as is the taste.

Keep it in a cool and dark place and it should last for well over a year, unless you eat it all in the meantime.

Note - You will have a better chutney if the cabbage is chopped very small; I use a food processor to achieve this.

SWEET TOMATO RELISH

I found this recipe tucked into one of my cookbooks, scribbled down on a piece of paper, but who gave it to me I do not know. Whoever did, I thank you for it. It has proved very popular with my customers. I do not know whether it is the colour or because it is "sweet" that makes it so popular.

If you have a surplus of red tomatoes or, indeed, if you are lucky enough to be given a quantity, then this relish is well worth doing as it is quite simple and does not take long too make. I put my surplus tomatoes from the greenhouse straight into a polythene bag and into the freezer, and when I have enough to work with I will bring them out, frozen, as they are much easier to skin. Just drop them one at a time into a bowl of hot water and the skins will just rub off!

You will need

3 lbs of ripe tomatoes
½ lb of onions, chopped into small pieces
1 large red pepper, de-seeded, and cut into ¼ inch squares
3 large stalks of celery cut in four lengthwise and then cut across the grain into small pieces
1 teaspoon of salt
½ pint of white spiced vinegar
¾ lb of white sugar
1 oz of rice flour, if you like a thicker relish
¼ teaspoon of hot chilli powder (optional)

SWEET TOMATO RELISH

Method

When you have prepared all the ingredients put all except the sugar and half of the vinegar, in an aluminium pan.

Bring to the boil and maintain at a simmer point for about 30 minutes or until the tomatoes have broken down to a pulp.

Add the sugar (and the chilli powder, if you want a more spicy relish). Boil for a further 10 minutes.

If you want to thicken the mixture, mix the rice flour with the remaining vinegar and add to the pan; otherwise add the remaining vinegar to the contents of the pan. Cook for a further 10 minutes.

Ladle the relish into clean dry jars and seal with a good airtight lid.

This will make about five pounds of relish, which is delicious when eaten with hamburgers or other similar meats. It can be eaten straight away but will keep for up to a year if stored correctly. Children love this recipe, as it is not too spicy for them (so take care with the chilli!).

Note: I use rice flour as a thickening agent in any chutney that tends towards being "runny". It is gluten free and therefore is acceptable to anyone who is allergic to wheat products.

GAMEKEEPER'S RELISH

CHUTNEYS

Yet another recipe that was generated by a customer's casual remark. "Well!" they said, "If you're going to have a Poacher's Pickle at least you should have a Gamekeeper's Relish!" A valid comment, and one that sent my inventive nature off into overdrive.

If the poacher was dark then the gamekeeper had to be light. What would complement the other's taste and yet still taste good with the same meats. This was the challenge and so I created this relish and offered it to my public and, as ever, kept asking for comments from the first few customers.

The first one that I asked came back instantly with the comment, "I won't wait till I get home!" and promptly opened the jar and did the finger test. His face said that I had "got it good" and the fact that he came back a couple of weeks later for two more jars told me that I had again struck oil - if you know what I mean.

You will need

1 large lemon, de-seeded
½ pint of water
2 ozs of root ginger
½ lb of onions
½ lb of skinned red tomatoes*
6 ozs of celery
½ pint of spiced vinegar
½ large red pepper, de-seeded
½ teaspoon of salt
¾ lb of sugar
1 tablespoon of arrowroot, mixed in 2 fl ozs of vinegar, to thicken the relish, when it is nearly ready.

GAMEKEEPER'S RELISH

Method

Cook the lemon in the water until the shell is soft and then discard any pips.

Homogenize this mix in a food processor and then put it in an aluminum pan. Grate the ginger; chop the onions and tomatoes, then add these and the vinegar to the pan. Bring the contents to the boil and maintain it at a steady simmer for about 10 minutes. Chop the celery into small cubes, (about ¼ of an inch or so) and add it to the simmering mixture in the pan. Add the salt and maintain the temperature for about 20 minutes. Add the sugar and bring it back to the boil for about 10 minutes. Chop the pepper into small cubes and add to the mixture. Bring to the boil and add sufficient of the arrowroot in vinegar, to thicken the mixture. Do not overcook at this stage or you will lose the effect of the peppers.

Carefully ladle into clean dry jars and seal with an airtight lid. This quantity makes about 3 lb of pale orange relish. Try it with cold meats - it is delicious.

This relish will be ready to eat about a week or so after it is made, but will improve for keeping.

It will keep for a year or more if kept cool and dark.

**Note: - A variation on the above is to make it with cranberries in place of the tomatoes, 6 ozs of fresh, or frozen, cranberries, together with half a pint of cranberry juice. This makes a pretty, pink relish that is a good complement to the dark Poacher's pickle when placed together on the table. Perhaps the poacher and the gamekeeper would not be seen together, even on the festive table!*

A COLLECTION OF OLD FASHIONED JELLIES

These four recipes can be modified according to your whim at the time.
The processes will work equally well whatever jelly you want to make: it depends which fruit you have available and what you want it to complement. A pure jelly is a beautiful clear preserve which can be served with many meats but often complements one in particular. I have a friend who likened them to stained glass windows with the sun shining through ... a beautiful description!
One of the features that endear these to me is that the fruits are readily available and will cost you nothing.

1) Crab Apple Jelly, which complements white meats and particularly pork. This is one of the oldest and yet it is the least made jelly. So many people remember it from their childhood, but have very little idea of what a crab apple looks like, let alone how you turn those little sour fruits into a lovely pink jelly. I did once try making it with the yellow crab apples in the hope that I could get a yellow jelly but it still turned out pink! Friends have crab apple trees for their blossom in the spring which creates the apples in the autumn; generally these same friends are only too willing to let you pick them; by the bucketful!
They are worth watching so that you get them before the birds.

2) Cydonium Jelly, made from quince. Real quince is not readily available but the fruit of the Quince-Japonica works equally well and is also the result of beautiful spring time blossom; the fruits are generally left to fall ... in the Fall! So find someone with a Quince tree or Japonica bush and offer to collect the fruits with the barter of a jar of jelly when it is made!

A COLLECTION OF OLD FASHIONED JELLIES

3) Rowan Jelly, a delicious complement to game particularly venison. Rowans are there for the collecting but you have to be smart to beat the birds. I try to watch the trees and as soon as the birds start getting interested in the berries I know it is time to go a-scrum ping. Collect more than you need. Carefully wash and de-stalk the rowans, making sure that there are no earwigs and other creepy-crawlies lurking amongst the berries you have collected. Any fruit that you do not use will freeze in a plastic bag.

4) Medlar Jelly ,will complement any cold meat. Medlars are a strange looking fruit (rather like a large blown up, brown, rose-hip) found in many old gardens but you have to wait until they are ready to fall off the tree before they are ready for use. The term for this is "bletted". This means that the fruits are soft to the touch and almost rotten, but not quite mouldy. You can collect them from the orchard floor but that harvest usually includes a share of grass, so it is better to select from the tree, if you can be patient to feel each fruit before you pick it.

You will need

1 lb of sugar for every pint of fruit stock*

A COLLECTION OF OLD FASHIONED JELLIES

Method

Make your fruit stock as given below and measure it into an aluminium preserving pan. Add sufficient sugar and bring to the boil. Keep it at a fast boil until you can achieve a good set.
Pour the jelly into clean dry jars and seal immediately.
1 pint for every 1 lb of sugar will make about a pound and a half of jelly; making in larger quantities is more efficient and will give you some for the stock cupboard .... and some surplus to give to friends!
It will keep for about a year if you store the finished jelly in a cold, dark place.
As with all jellies you will need to watch the pan and to stir it almost continuously otherwise a bubbly scum will be produced which is difficult to disperse; you can carefully lift it off with a strainer spoon but it is better to avoid its acquisition and not have the problem.

You can add spices, particularly cinnamon or nutmeg, to the jelly as it cooks (add a little at a time until the taste is right), put in a small quantity of chilli seeds or try putting a few geranium leaves in with the crab apples; such variations make an ordinary jelly intriguing.

*To make the stock-
for *crab apple*, cut the fruits through to make sure that there are no maggots or bugs inside.
for *quince*, cut the fruit into cubes about the size of the top of your thumb.
for *rowan*, you will need equal weights of rowans and apples, which are cut into small cubes.

for *medlar*, check the fruits for any that show signs of mould and discard these.

Put the fruit in a large pan and just cover with water. Simmer for 2½ to 3 hours. If you have a lid to the pan so much the better but if not cover the pan with cling film making two small holes in to stop it blowing its top. When you have a deep pink liquor pour the whole contents of the pan into a strainer and allow to drain overnight.

With medlars, cover the fruit with water and smash them as they cook, strain the contents of your pan into a large bowl but return the residue to the pan. Cover this residue with water and re-boil, again working the fruit through the water. Strain this into the bowl. You may have to repeat this procedure a third time but finally strain all the collected liquid in the bowl through a fine metal or muslin sieve leaving it to drain through, preferably overnight.

The liquid obtained is a muddy-brown at this stage.

Any surplus fruit stock can be poured into plastic bottles and stored in the freezer; so it is worth making plenty to have some surplus to make up at a later date.

My tip is to label your bottles of stock with the date and type, as it is almost impossible to distinguish one from another once they are frozen. I once ended up with a mixture of grape and quince juice but I had poured them in to the pan before I realised my mistake; it was a good, if strange, combination!

MINT IN APPLE JELLY (OR ROSEMARY JELLY)

Not strictly a jelly, although it did start off like one, but I found that by using the flesh of the apple I ended up with a tracklement that would complement both lamb and pork. quite apart from other foods.

I know of one young lady, who can not eat new potatoes without it! No accounting for the uses that some folks will make of a jelly.

The rosemary Jelly is made in the same way but, whereas with mint the flavours complement the apple, with rosemary the herb totally overrides the taste. Pick the non flowering shoots of rosemary and serve your jelly with roast Lamb. It is delicious!

You will need

4½ lbs of prepared cooking apples, requires approximately 5½ lbs of apples
4½ lbs of sugar
1½ pints of water
1 pint of white spiced vinegar
3 heaped tablespoons of chopped mint (or rosemary)**

MINT IN APPLE JELLY (OR ROSEMARY JELLY)

Method

Peel and core the apples then cut them into quarters. Put the peelings and cores in a saucepan with ½ pint of water and cook for about 25 minutes. Meanwhile put the quartered apples in a preserving pan (with a lid, if possible) and cook them very gently until they are fluffy. Mash the apples thoroughly with a potato masher.
Rub the peel and cores through a metal sieve into the preserving pan with the back of a wooden spoon, this helps to colour "green" the final preserve.
Add the vinegar and sugar to the pan and then boil rapidly until you get a good set. Keep an eye on it or it will turn pink. The colour does not alter the flavour but I like to keep it green, if possible.
When you are satisfied with the set, add the chopped mint, (or rosemary) but make sure that the mixture is still at boiling point. Quickly pour into clean dry jars and seal.

This will make about eight pounds of jelly that will keep for a year, if kept cool and dark. It does tend to lose its green colour with time but that does not alter the flavour.

* *This can be made with apples that are taken off the tree, early, to facilitate the rest growing bigger as the autumn proceeds. They are probably too small to peel but if you cut them through into quarters (to check that they are sound inside) and cook them in the water for about 40 minutes - then rub them through a metal sieve into the preserving pan, adding the vinegar and continuing as above. The result is a beautiful bright green preserve, which uses apples which otherwise might be composted .*

** *If I do not have fresh mint in the garden, I use 3 teaspoonsfuls of commercial bottled garden mint. That's a cheat but the green is more emphasised, and it is equally good!*

CHILLI JELLI

I often wonder what prompts people to come up with comments like "Have you ever thought of making Chilli Jam?" Thought of it... I had not even heard of it!

Was this being done to try to wrong foot me or was it to test my skills and innovation? Whatever the reason was, it was enough of a challenge for me. When my neighbour passed this thought across my table, I asked her what she meant by Chilli Jam and then started trying to piece together what might have gone into it as well as chillies. They are hardly the stuff from which to make jam! They are long red things that will make your fingers burn if you do not work sufficiently quickly with the raw fruit! However, having discussed what you would eat it with and what it looked like, I had a good idea of how to try to make it. I made a very small quantity and passed it next door for her approval.
I got the thumbs up from my tasters so I have added it to the range, but I have called it Chilli Jelli. It is definitely not a jam!

You will need

¾ pint of apple juice*
1 red chilli
¼ pint water
1 level teaspoonful of red chilli powder
1 lemon
¼ teaspoon of chilli seeds
¾ lb sugar

CHILLI JELLI

Method

Quarter the lemon and cook it for about 45 minutes in the water, be careful that it does not boil dry while you are waiting for the shell to soften. When the lemon is soft put it in a liquidiser with the liquid in which it is cooked and whiz until it is smooth.

Carefully slice the chilli across (to make thin rings).

Put it into an aluminium pan with the apple juice, the chilli seeds and chilli powder and the lemon puree.

Bring to the boil and maintain the temperature for about 15 minutes.

Add the sugar, raise the temperature and boil for a further 5 minutes when you should get a good set, and it should be a beautiful deep pink.

Let the jelli cool a little and stir before pouring it into clean dry jars. Seal and store in a cool dark place.

This should make a couple of pound jars but I would advise bottling in smaller jars as you can then keep it for a year or more without it losing its glorious colour. Of course, you can double up the quantities too, but I would not advise eating twice as much as it is rather lethal! An excellent dip for plain crackers.

** To make a very useful "apple juice", chop a quantity of apples, you can use windfalls or apples that are less than perfect, include the cores and skin but make sure that there are no bugs in the middle if they are "rejects". Cover the apples with water and boil for about 45 minutes then pour the entire contents into a metal sieve and collect the juice that drips through. This juice can be used, as above, as it will be rich in pectin.*

BEETROOT MARMALADE

Another enigma that really confuses people because they cannot get away from the thought that Marmalade has to be made with oranges. This marmalade includes beetroot and it is not eaten on toast at breakfast. The recipe was one that I had heard of and thus my imagination was inspired to try to create something that lived up to the name.

The result is an odd combination that works on the level of strange tastes that complement each other.

Eat this marmalade with goat's cheese or with some deep fried Brie, and with fingers of toast or crisp breads; add a crisp green salad ...absolutely delicious!
Serve it as a starter and watch your guest's faces change from consternation to delight. Hide the remainder of your batch or your guests will be taking it home with them!

You will need

Two large oranges (about 1¼lbs)
1¼ lbs of cooked beetroot
1 pint of water
½ pint of white spiced vinegar
2 lbs of white sugar
4 ozs sultanas
½ teaspoon of caraway seeds
½ teaspoon of pimento and eight cloves, all ground together in a mortar and pestle
¼ teaspoonful of salt
¼ teaspoonful of ground, white pepper

BEETROOT MARMALADE

Method

Cut the oranges lengthwise into eight strips and then chop them across into thin chunks. Put them into a pan, with the water, and cook them for about 45 minutes to soften the peel.
Skin the beetroot and chop them very small, using a food processor, add these to the oranges along with the vinegar and the remaining ingredients, except the sugar. Bring back to a gentle boil and maintain the temperature for a further 30 minutes. This allows the oranges to absorb the colour from the beetroot and the sultanas to swell.
Add the sugar and bring back to boiling point for a further 30 minutes. Keep the marmalade stirred, and should it become dry, add a little more liquid (half water: half vinegar).
Spoon the mixture into clean dry jars and seal them immediately.

This will make about six pounds of an excellent tracklement. It will store for about a year but do keep it cool and dark to maintain the colour.

HEDGEROW JELLY

This is a jelly that can be made for just the price of the sugar if you make the time to go out into the country lanes and find the fruits of autumn.

You will need

Use a combination of:-
Rosehips,
Elderberries
and
Blackberries, but you can also add Sloes, if you can find them, in the countryside.

HEDGEROW JELLY

Method

You need to prepare each fruit on its own, then combine your extracted stock before you add the sugar* and proceed as for any of the jellies above.
I use ¼ pint of each of the rosehip and elderberry along with ½ pint of blackberry juice to each pound of sugar, but you can vary the amount of each according to your taste or indeed according to the relative abundance of each fruit.
Rosehips are very hard and need chopping - I use my food processor - before they are cooked. Barely cover the broken fruits with water and cook for about 45 minutes, then squeeze through a sieve.
With both the elderberries and the blackberries add about half as much water as fruit, bring to the boil, cook for about 20 minutes then rub the contents of the pan through a sieve to extract as much flesh off the seeds as possible (discard the seeds). If you are using sloes again use half the volume of water, cook and rub through a sieve.
This will make an excellent complement to ice cream or yogurt or spread it on fresh bread.

**using Jam or Pectin sugar you get a quicker set and a firmer preserve.*

LIME MARMALADE

Early in my jam making career I was fortunate to be living in the West Indies. At that time I had heard of limes but had no experience of their taste, let alone know what to do with them. Knowing that I had made marmalade with green oranges, I was given a large bag of limes by a Jamaican fellow with the comment, "Can you do something with these?"

"I'll try," was my reply. I remember the conversation but have no memory of making the marmalade except for the taste of it. I can now never cut a lime without being reminded of it and I am always surprised, even now, as I was then, by the difference between my marmalade and the commercial variety.

Nowadays limes are readily available in most supermarkets. Choose ones with dark green hulls, but be prepared, the greener they are the harder they are to cut and subsequently soften!

You will need

12 - 14 limes and 2 good sized lemons. This should yield about 3 lbs of fruit, in weight
4 pints of water
5 lbs of sugar

(Adjust the amount of water and sugar depending upon the weight of the fruit)

LIME MARMALADE

Method

Cut the limes into four, lengthwise, and slice across as thinly as possible. Cut the lemons into six, lengthwise, and slice across as thinly as possible.
Put the cut fruit into a copper* preserving pan with the water.
Bring to the boil and maintain a good simmer for at least 45 minutes to soften the hulls of the fruit.
If you have reduced the amount of liquid in the pan, due to the time it has taken to achieve this, then add a little more water.

Add the sugar and cook for a further 15 to 20 minutes. Test a little of the liquid on a cold saucer to see if it wrinkles, but you should get a very reliable set.

This will make about 12 lbs of the most aristocratic of marmalades, which will keep for up to a year if you store it in a cold dark place: that is if you manage not to eat it all beforehand.

Notes
The copper pan is the secret for maintaining the colour of the limes. An aluminium pan will not alter the flavour but the marmalade does lose its glorious green colour.

If you have a shredder or a food processor this will take the work out of cutting the fruit.

"NO BITS" MARMALADE

I had tried making jelly marmalade by straining out the bits for those who did not like them but always felt that I was throwing the best part of the marmalade away. I had one little lad come to my stall one day and while his Mum was buying a "proper" marmalade, he said to me "Ugh! I don't like the bits".

That was enough to set my mind ticking and I decided to try homogenizing the fruit before I added the sugar.
Bingo! A full fruit marmalade, without the bits, was the result!

I have told the story of the little lad many times to people who are intrigued by the title of the marmalade and invariably I get the comment, "I've got a big boy who doesn't like the bits!" Needless to say the name creates a lot of interest and a little laughter, and I am still amazed that it is not available commercially, as it is a very satisfying full fruit marmalade but without any bits!

You will need

1 large grapefruit
2 large lemons
½ lb of (prepared) Seville Oranges
4 lbs of sugar
2½ pints of water

"NO BITS" MARMALADE

Method

Cut the fruit into quarters removing the pips.*
Cook gently in a pint of water for about 45 minutes. Put all this into a liquidiser or Food processor and homogenise the fruit.
Return the liquidised fruit to the pan, add a further pint (and a half, if needed) of water and the sugar. Bring to the boil and maintain this for about 30 minutes when you should get a good set.

Pour into clean dry jars and seal immediately.

This should make seven to eight pounds of marmalade that does not have any bits.
It will keep for a year or more, providing it is stored in a cool and dark place.

** Note - The pips are a rich source of pectin and should be incorporated into the liquid that is used in the making of the marmalade. There are various ways of doing this. Here are three suggestions.*

i I put the pips in a pan and boil them separately in some of the water for about 45 minutes and then strain them out using the resulting "juice" as part of the liquid added to the liquidised fruit. Some extra water may be needed if boiling the "skins" has reduced the quantity.

ii If I have time, I cook the fruit and pips together in the same pan until the fruit is soft and then leave it to cool when I can take the pips out, by hand, before liquidising the fruit.

iii Some folk put the pips in a muslin bag and place this in the original boiling of the fruit and then remove the bag when the fruit is cooked. The important thing is not to discard them until you have extracted all of the pectin that they contain.

DARK AND STORMY (AND GINGER) MARMALADE

The idea for this marmalade came to me when I was visiting Bermuda.
This name is not only used for my marmalade but, in Bermuda, it is also a drink and one of the specialities at the Swizzle Inn. I have to this day, a sweat shirt that bears the legend "Swizzle Inn: Stagger out" that I got when I visited there. A nice little joke!

I always know when a customer has also been to the islands as their face lights up at the sheer mention of the name.

It is quite a spectacular marmalade and once tried, you will come back again and again for more. It is always a good talking point as the explanation of how it is made will always intrigue the listener. All at breakfast, as offered by me.

You will need

1 lb of prepared Seville Oranges
1 prepared large lemon
3 ozs of root ginger
3 heaped teaspoons of chopped, crystallised ginger
1½ dessert spoons of black treacle
4 fl ozs of good quality rum, I use Appleton Gold, a Special Jamaican Rum. Alternatively, one of the best I have found is Gosling (Bermuda) Black Seal Rum.
3 lbs of sugar
1 pint of water

DARK AND STORMY (AND GINGER) MARMALADE

Method

Grate the root ginger, and chop the crystallised ginger into small pieces.
Prepare the Seville oranges and lemons as you do for **ST CLEMENTS**.

Put all these ingredients into a preserving pan with the water and cook gently for about 45 minutes until the skins are soft.
Add the sugar and boil for a further 30 minutes or until you get a good set.
Add the treacle, stir well to mix and bring back to the boil for a further 2 or 3 minutes.
Switch off the heat and leave it for about half-an-hour stirring occasionally.
When deemed cool enough add the rum, thoroughly stir it in. Pour into clean dry jars and seal immediately.

This will make about five or six pounds of a brilliant marmalade.
If you can bear to keep it, the marmalade does improve and will keep for a year if kept cool and dark.
The ginger matures with time and consequently the longer it is left, the fuller is the taste.

This is probably my most popular marmalade.

To make a **GINGER MARMALADE** use the above recipe but omit the treacle and the rum.

MYRA MARMALADE

This recipe was one that I created as a special fundraiser for our local church's tower restoration project. The church is in the village of Earl's Croome located in south Worcestershire and is named after St Nicholas.
I wanted to create a marmalade that was different to all the others that I had made. It had to be sufficiently innovative to encourage visitors to want to buy it when they were visiting our exhibition. Not only did I have to devise it but I also had to come up with a name that was both intriguing and yet was relevant to what we were doing with the exhibition.

This wonderful, three fruit marmalade was the result.

As the church's patron saint is St Nicholas' (he of Santa Claus fame) and as history, or legend, has it, he was also the patron of "threes" and was also the Bishop of Myra, during the fourth century, it all fitted together and a new marmalade was born with a story that justifies its existence.

It has proved popular; unfortunately, folk still think my name is Myra, even after I explain the tale.

You will need

One grapefruit, Three lemons, Five limes
(The fruits for each of these ingredients should weigh about a pound. The closer you can get to equal weights of the three fruits, the better will be your marmalade.)
3 pints of water
4½ lbs of sugar

MYRA MARMALADE

Method

Thinly slice all the fruit. I use the slicing feature on my food processor but you can, with patience, cut by hand. Limes are hard to cut so you will need a good sharp knife and be careful!
Put it all in a copper* preserving pan with the water and bring to the boil.
Simmer for about 45 minutes until all the hulls are soft, particularly the limes.
If you do have a lid to your pan this will stop the water boiling off, but watch the level and top it up with a little more water, if necessary.
Add the sugar, raise the temperature and boil the mixture gently for a further 20 minutes when you should then get a good set. Turn the heat up for the last couple of minutes to get a good boil through the marmalade.

Pour into clean dry jars and seal.
This will make about nine pounds of a deliciously sharp and interesting marmalade.

It will keep for at least a year but do keep it cool and in a dark place as this will preserve the beautiful colour, which is a delightful yellow with deep green bits within it.

** The use of a copper pan enables the limes to stay green. If you do not have one of these then use an ordinary aluminium pan. The marmalade will taste just as good even though the limes will have lost some of their colour.*

ST CLEMENTS MARMALADE

I wonder how many times I have been asked, "Why is it called 'St Clements'?" The nursery rhyme of the same name often answers the question. This marmalade is simply a hybrid of the two fruits.
A delightful marmalade that is not as strong as a conventional Seville and yet is very fruity. You can adjust the relative quantities of the two fruits but my preference is to have equal amounts.

You will need

1 lb of Seville oranges	**1 lb of lemons**
4¼ lb of sugar	**2½ pints of water**

Method

Cut the Seville oranges in half and remove all the pips. Place the pips in a separate saucepan and simmer them for 45 minutes in about 1 pint of the water. Leave in the saucepan for the pips to settle. Thinly slice the oranges and lemons, place in a preserving pan with the rest of the water and simmer gently for about 45 minutes.
Carefully decant the liquid off the pips and add to the preserving pan.
Add the sugar to the pan and boil for about 30 minutes until a good set is achieved.
Pour into clean dry jars and seal quickly.

This will make about 8 lbs of marmalade that will keep for a year if kept cool and dark. If you want to vary the quantities of oranges and lemons, a good rule of thumb is to use about 3 lbs of sugar to each pound of Sevilles and 1¼ lbs for each pound of lemons.

GRAPEFRUIT OR LEMON MARMALADE

Both of these are very simple marmalades but they do offer a different approach to the more conventional marmalades that are made with Oranges. Some folk seem to be allergic to Oranges yet they can tolerate other citrus fruits, so these will fit well in their diet. I offer them more as something tasty and quite different to the accepted norm.

You will need

3 lbs of fruit:
For grapefruit marmalade; I use two large yellow grapefruits and two large lemons
For the lemon marmalade; make your weight up by just using lemons
3 pints of water
4 lbs of sugar

Method

Slice the fruit thinly. I use the slicing gadget on my food processor.
Put all the fruit in a large jelly pan* with the water, bring to the boil and simmer for about 45 minutes to soften the peel.
When it is soft add the sugar, raise the temperature and simmer for about 30 minutes. Test for a set. When you are almost satisfied raise the temperature and give the marmalade a fast boil for about three minutes.
Pour into clean dry jars and seal immediately.

FIVE FRUIT SHRED

In one of the houses in which I lived, we had a big garden. In this garden I had planted a mini orchard with all sorts of fruit trees, including three different types of pears.

Once I had an absolute glut of the fruits and tried out various ideas I had as to how to use them, rather than leaving them for the birds!

There are only so many ways in which pears can normally be used, so I sought another.

Pears do not contain much pectin but do have a distinctive flavour. I decided to try them out with a high pectin fruit, namely apples, and added them to the conventional three fruits that make another popular marmalade.

Bingo! A thick, flavourful, sweet marmalade! You can even use bottled or canned pears but fresh fruit does give the best flavour.

You will need

1 large grapefruit
3 large dessert oranges
2 large (or 3 small) lemons
1 lb of cooking apples
1 lb of pears (Conference variety give the best result but any other variety of pear will do)
2½ pints of water
6 lbs of sugar

FIVE FRUIT SHRED

Method

Prepare the citrus fruits by slicing them thinly and put the slices in a large jelly pan.
Peel and core the apples and pears. Cook the peel and cores, separately, in ½ pint of water. When soft push through a metal sieve into the pan containing the sliced citrus fruits (discard the residue).
Add the remainder of the water and bring to boiling point.
Roughly chop the apples and pears and add these to the pan. Return to boiling point and cook all the fruit slowly for about 45 minutes, or until the citrus peel is soft.*
Add the sugar, stir well and maintain at a gentle boil for a further 30 minutes. This allows the flavours to meld together.*

Boil rapidly for about five minutes and test for a set.

When you are satisfied with the set, pour the marmalade into clean dry jars and seal immediately.

This will make about eleven pounds of a first class marmalade that will keep for a year if kept cool and dark. It particularly appeals to those who like a thick, sweet marmalade on their toast in the morning.

**If you have a lid to your preserving pan this will stop evaporation during the slow cooking time: if not, and it is needed, add a little more water so that your marmalade does not become dry.*

THREE FRUIT MARMALADE

This is extremely popular and has the advantage that it can be made at any time of year because citrus fruit is always available and thus does not have to be made in the "Seville season". I was first shown how to make it by a little old lady who had made it all her life. She must have been in her eighties then so I think that it can be considered as one of the traditional marmalades. Strangely, my customers see it as a fancy marmalade, I would rather say that it was a reliable marmalade.

You will need

1 large Grapefruit
2 large dessert oranges
2 large lemons
4 ¼ lbs of sugar
3 pints of water

THREE FRUIT MARMALADE

Method

Prepare the fruit by slicing it into half-inch strips, lengthwise, and then cut across as finely as you can manage.*
Put the cut fruit into the pan with the water.

Bring contents of the pan to the boil and maintain it at simmer point for about 45 minutes.

Add the sugar and boil for about 30 minutes or until you get a good set.

Pour into clean dry jars and seal.

This will make seven to eight pounds of marmalade that will keep for a year or more providing you keep it cool and dark.

**Alternatively, put them through a slicing machine. This will reduce the labour of preparation. Another option is to chop or mince the fruit. This is easier but it does not produce such a good- looking marmalade.*

Note -
If you can leave the cut fruit to steep, overnight, it will make the process of softening the fruit easier. I often cook it and leave overnight, adding the sugar in the morning.

WHISKY MARMALADE

I always say this is for the Teachers' fans. I think originally this marmalade inherited its subtitle from the fact that I was a teacher, but for a laugh I make it with the celebrated scotch whisky. A good play on words.
Therefore, it got a "double whammy" and one that inevitably provokes some comment.
Were it to obey modern legislation it would have to be labelled as, an 'Orange marmalade with Whisky, but that does not have quite the same ring to it, neither would it provoke the comments that I get from the public.

This is probably the most popular marmalade of my range as I certainly always seem to be making it.

You will need

2 lbs of Seville oranges
2 large lemons
6 lbs of Sugar
2 pints of water
8 tablespoonfuls of whisky

To make a **SEVILLE MARMALADE** *, I call it the "boring" one of the range, follow the above recipe but omit the whisky and bottle the mixture as soon as you are satisfied with the set.*

Method

Prepare the Seville oranges by cutting them in half and removing the pips. Boil the pips in about ¾ pint of the water for about 45 minutes. Leave them for a few minutes to settle then decant the liquid off into your preserving pan. Discard the pips.

WHISKY MARMALADE

Method (contd)

Slice the fruit as thinly as possible, add it all to the preserving pan with the rest of the water. Bring to the boil, and simmer for about 45 minutes to soften the hulls of the fruit. Add the sugar, raise the temperature to bring the marmalade back to boiling point and maintain this for a further 45 minutes.
Test for a set.
When you are satisfied with the set, raise the temperature and give your marmalade a brisk boil for 3 to 5 minutes. This should have two effects, it will make the set harder but also it will mean that your marmalade will keep longer. Turn off the heat and leave the marmalade to cool for 30 minutes. The length of time does depend on the temperature of your kitchen. You need to make sure that the marmalade is not too hot, as the alcohol will fizz off, neither should it be too cool which will reduce the "keeping" life of the finished marmalade. Experiment with a little whisky at first and you will soon get the hang of the timing! Stir the marmalade, add the whisky and stir well to mix them thoroughly. Quickly pour the mixture into clean, dry jars and seal immediately.

This quantity will make about eleven pounds of marmalade that will keep (cool and dark) for a year - providing you do not eat it in the meantime. The quality does not deteriorate with time as the whisky is integrated with the marmalade and not just poured on the top.

PUCKRUP MARMALADE

Folk always read this as "pickup" and as it is a sharp marmalade they are probably not too far wrong. However, that is not the reason for its name.

Puckrup is a small hamlet on the Gloucestershire and Worcestershire border, lying on a hill to the east of the River Severn. The name means the den or home (rup) of the hobgoblins (Pucks).

When I first devised this marmalade, there was a danger that the hamlet and the name would disappear into obscurity. I wanted to keep the name alive and I also wanted a name for a new marmalade.

So the two desires that I had were married together. Fortunately the danger of annihilation of this hamlet passed. The 'big house' was renamed Puckrup Hall and is now, at the time of publication, an hotel.

This marmalade still creates such a problem for my customers that I have often thought that I ought to change the name, but then why let modernity destroy our heritage? In any case, a good yarn goes with a good marmalade; so Puckrup it has remained!

You will need

4 Limes
2 Lemons
1 Grapefruit
½ lb of Seville oranges
4½ lbs of sugar
3 pints of water

PUCKRUP MARMALADE

Method

Slice all the fruit as thinly as it is possible to do and cook it slowly for about 45 minutes in the water so as to soften all the rind.
If you have access to a copper jelly pan, you will be rewarded, as the lime hulls will stay green.
Add the sugar and stir it in, then raise the temperature to bring the mixture back to the boiling point.
Maintain at a simmer for a further 30 minutes when you should get a good set when the juice is tested. Boil rapidly for a further 2 minutes and then pour into clean dry jars and seal immediately.

This will make eight to nine pounds of a very reliable and tasty marmalade, which will keep for a year, providing you keep it in a cool dark place.

Note - The use of a copper pan enables the limes to stay green. If you do not have one of these then use an ordinary aluminium pan. The marmalade will taste just as good even though the limes will have lost some of their colour.

SWEET ORANGE IN COINTREAU

This is a very popular marmalade. It has a good thick texture that has the added kick of Cointreau. It always turns out a lovely deep orange and so looks good as well as tasting good.
I can remember one German lady insisting on coming to my house and selecting her way through every jar I had in the cupboard before she got the half-dozen that she deemed to be the best. It was difficult not to laugh as they were all made at the same time. However, things made by hand never do turn out identical!

You will need

3 large dessert oranges
2 large lemons
1½ lbs of prepared apples
5 lbs of sugar
3½ pints of water
10 tablespoons of Cointreau

SWEET ORANGE IN COINTREAU

Method

Prepare the citrus fruit as you would for making the three fruit marmalade, either by hand slicing or using a machine. Slice the apples, or cut them into very small pieces.

Put all of the fruit into an aluminium pan along with the water and cook gently until all the citrus fruit is softened and the apple has pulped. This will take about 45 minutes.

Add the sugar and boil until you get a good set, remembering that you are going to add a little more liquid to the final marmalade. This will take about 40 minutes.

When you are satisfied with your set, turn off the heat and leave the pan to stand for 20 to 30 minutes to allow the marmalade mixture to cool*.

Stir the marmalade occasionally to prevent a skin forming.

Add the Cointreau. Stir it in thoroughly and then pour the marmalade into clean, dry jars and seal as quickly as you can.

This will make about nine pounds of a deliciously different marmalade that will keep for a year, if it is somewhere cool and dark. It does improve - if it is not eaten straight away!

** The length of time that you leave it to cool depends on the temperature in your kitchen and the shape of your pan. Let it cool too much and you will reduce the "keep" ability of the marmalade; on the other hand if it is too hot the alcohol will fizzle off and you will lose some of the kick.*

RED ONION MARMALADE

I am always asked two questions with this one.
One is "Does it taste of onions?"; the other is "Is it eaten on toast, like a marmalade?"
The answer to both of these questions is "No!"

It is difficult to describe what the marmalade does actually taste of but certainly the red onions are sweeter and softer than ordinary onions and certainly there is no resemblance between this and conventional pickled onions.

You get an almost caramelised taste ,which is partly due to the combination of spices. I avoid answering the questions but offer the more positive comment that it is a brilliant complement to pate.
Personally, I like it with a coarse pate but it is good with any meat varieties.
Try it with a game pie, when served cold. It is excellent.

You will need

1½ lbs of red onions
½ teaspoon of salt
1 heaped teaspoon of caraway seeds
½ teaspoon of ground cloves or 20 cloves, ground in a pestle and mortar
1¼ lbs of white sugar
½ pint of white spiced vinegar

RED ONION MARMALADE

Method

Chop the onions. I use a food processor, and put these in an aluminium pan with the salt, spices and vinegar. Bring the mixture to the boil and simmer it slowly for about 45 minutes.

Add the sugar, then bring back to the boiling point and maintain the mixture at a simmer until the onions have become translucent, by which time most of the liquid will have been absorbed. This should take about an hour.
It is worth repeatedly stirring the mixture, during this time, as it may stick to you pan.

Do not over heat the mixture or you will lose the glorious colour.
When ready pour into clean dry jars and seal.

This will make about three pounds of “marmalade”.
It is ready to eat immediately but does improve with keeping. I tend to make a double batch and try to keep it. It will last for a twelve months, in theory!

THE TOOLS FOR THE JOB

As with all food preparation, ensure that all of your equipment is clean and the area in which you are working is hygienic before you start any cooking.

Jam making requires certain tools and equipment. Below is a list of those items that I feel are needed if you are about to become or already are a serious jam maker.

- A selection of good sharp knives, including a peeler.
- A good sized, aluminium jam pan, preferably with a lid.
- A copper jam pan.
- A good set of weighing scales.
- A microwave cooker; although not essential it makes sterilising jam jars a lot easier.
- A set of good measuring spoons.
- A set of good wooden spoons - keep some for jam and some for chutneys, so as not to get any cross contamination of flavours.
- A collection of jam jars in a variety of sizes, including some that have a one pound capacity.
- Sugar (or jam) thermometer.
- Food processor.
- Hand-held food blender.
- Good quality wire sieve.
- Potato "Masher".
- Mortar & Pestle
- Labels, for the jars, and jam pot covers and lids.
- A good large storage cupboard - you will need it!

Mrs G's Copper Jam Pan

Brass weights and a pivot scale, still used by Mrs G

Mortar & Pestle along with a selection of knives

Well-used wooden spoons used to stir the mixtures

Hexagonal Jam Jars

Round jars

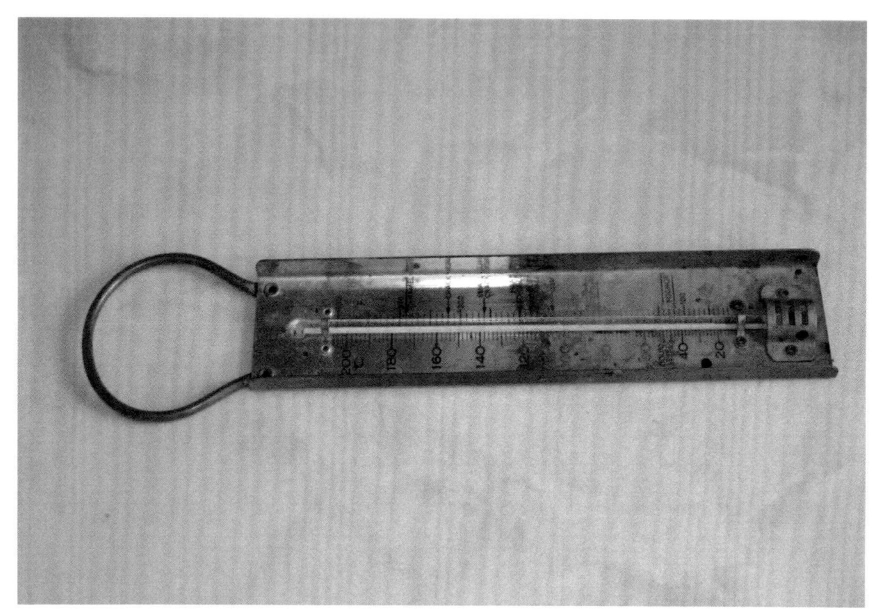

A sugar (Jam) thermometer

The end products ready to be enjoyed

CONTENTS

Notes

Notes